In the Midst of Events

The years 1950 and 1951 were important ones in post-war British foreign policy. The Cold War was at its height with the outbreak of the Korean War in June 1950 and the controversy over German rearmament. Britain's refusal in 1950 to join the Schuman Plan for a European Coal and Steel Community marked a crucial stage in the development of its subsequent European policy and the bitter dispute with the Iranian government over oil nationalisation which broke out in 1951 typified the challenge to its informal empire in the Middle East.

Kenneth Younger was the second-ranking minister in the Foreign Office under Ernest Bevin and Herbert Morrison from February 1950 until the Labour government's defeat in the general election of October 1951. His diaries and papers, published here for the first time, offer a unique insight into British and world politics at a time when Britain could still claim to be a world power. Younger's incisive analysis and vivid descriptions of events and personalities make this volume an essential primary source for anyone interested in the period, while his shrewd assessments of Britain's European policy and the 'special relationship' with the United States are as relevant today as they were more than half a century ago.

Geoffrey Warner was born in 1937 and studied history at Cambridge and political science in Paris. He has held university posts both in Britain and abroad, including four at professorial level. From 1993–2002 he was first College Lecturer and then Supernumerary Fellow in Modern History at Brasenose College, Oxford. He first met Kenneth Younger while working for him at the Royal Institute of International Affairs (Chatham House) in 1961–3.

British politics and society
Series editor: Peter Catterall
ISSN: 1467–1441

Social change impacts not just upon voting behaviour and party identity but also the formulation of policy. But how do social changes and political developments interact? Which shapes which? Reflecting a belief that social and political structures cannot be understood either in isolation from each other or from the historical processes which form them, this series will examine the forces that have shaped British society. Cross-disciplinary approaches will be encouraged. In the process, the series will aim to make a contribution to existing fields, such as politics, sociology and media studies, as well as opening out new and hitherto-neglected fields.

The Making of Channel 4
Edited by Peter Catterall

Managing Domestic Dissent in First World War Britain
Brock Millman

Reforming the Constitution
Debates in twenty-first century Britain
Edited by Peter Catterall, Wolfram Kaiser and Ulrike Walton-Jordan

Pessimism and British War Policy, 1916–1918
Brock Millman

Amateurs and Professionals in Post-war British Sport
Edited by Adrian Smith and Dilwyn Porter

A Life of Sir John Eldon Gorst
Disraeli's awkward disciple
Archie Hunter

Conservative Party Attitudes to Jews, 1900–1950
Harry Defries

Poor Health
Social inequality before and after the Black Report
Edited by Virginia Berridge and Stuart Blume

Mass Conservatism
The Conservatives and the public since the 1880s
Edited by Stuart Ball and Ian Holliday

Defining British Citizenship
Empire, Commonwealth and modern Britain
Rieko Karatani

Television policies of the Labour Party, 1951–2001
Des Freedman

Creating the National Health Service
Aneurin Bevan and the medical Lords
Marvin Rintala

A Social History of Milton Keynes
Middle England/edge city
Mark Clapson

Scottish Nationalism and the Idea of Europe
Atsuko Ichijo

The Royal Navy in the Falklands Conflict and the Gulf War
Culture and strategy
Alastair Finlan

The Labour Party in Opposition 1970–1974
Prisoners of history
Patrick Bell

The Civil Service Commission, 1855–1991
A bureau biography
Richard A. Chapman

Popular Newspapers, the Labour Party and British Politics
James Thomas

In the Midst of Events
The Foreign Office diaries and papers of Kenneth Younger,
February 1950–October 1951
Geoffrey Warner

In the Midst of Events

The Foreign Office diaries and papers
of Kenneth Younger,
February 1950–October 1951

Geoffrey Warner

 Routledge
Taylor & Francis Group

LONDON AND NEW YORK

First published 2005
by Routledge
2 Park Square, Milton Park, Abingdon, Oxon OX14 4RN

Simultaneously published in the USA and Canada
by Routledge
711 Third Avenue, New York, NY 10017

Routledge is an imprint of the Taylor & Francis Group

Transferred to Digital Printing 2005

Typeset in Garamond by Wearset Ltd, Boldon, Tyne and Wear

British Library Cataloguing in Publication Data
A catalogue record for this book is available from the British Library

Library of Congress Cataloging in Publication Data
A catalog record for this book has been requested

First issued in paperback 2013

ISBN 13: 978-0-714-65622-9 (hbk)
ISBN 13: 978-0-415-84891-6 (pbk)

To my extended family
Ronnie, Frances/Kris, Brian, Sophie, Stefan, Adam and Zoë

Contents

General editor's preface   x
Acknowledgements   xii
Editorial principles   xiii
Abbreviations   xiv

Introduction   1

1 To the Foreign Office, February–August 1950   7

2 The United Nations, September–December 1950   33

3 From Bevin to Morrison, January–March 1951   52

4 The end of the Labour government, April–October 1951   72

Appendix   97
Notes   102
Index   119

General editor's preface

Kenneth Younger never quite attained the first-class political status which goes with Cabinet rank. However he was able, during the eighteen months or so covered by this edition of his diaries, to influence the conduct of British diplomacy, particularly during the lengthy illness that marked the closing stages of Ernest Bevin's tenure as Foreign Secretary. In their course, as well, he proves an acute observer of the difficulties facing the Attlee government at that time, not least in the international arena. Naturally, the problem of confronting or containing the communist threat looms particularly large in his account. It is interesting to observe that Younger, after discussing the Schuman Plan for a European Coal and Steel Community and the British alternatives to it, soon notes that 'The Korean situation has now knocked Schuman right into the background of public consciousness'. Other foreign policy problems are certainly mentioned, particularly the lengthy Abadan crisis in 1951, occasioned by the Iranian attempt to nationalise the British oil assets in their country. But the theme which dominates these pages is the Cold War and the question, made more acute by the Korean War, of how the western powers should respond to both the Soviet Union and China.

Whilst Younger's entries evoke the tensions of those years, they do so from a very considered perspective. The sense of crisis, of the need to confront communist aggression, is clearly recorded. But Younger was a critical and dispassionate observer of such anxieties. Even more than a commentary on the early stages of the Cold War, this diary offers an insider's account of the stresses and strains resulting in the Anglo-American alliance. A contemporary diarist on the other side of the House of Commons, the future Conservative Prime Minister Harold Macmillan, felt at the time that the record was one generally of craven surrender to the Americans by the Labour government of which Younger was a part. Interestingly, Younger is also critical, but on rather different grounds. So, for instance, whilst Macmillan was very dismissive of Attlee's visit to Washington in December 1950, prompted by fears that the US might use the atomic bomb over Korea, Younger felt that the trip was a success. His complaint was more that the American prosecution of the Cold War was at time unnecessarily aggressive, if not provocative, and that his superiors in government either could not or would not do enough to rein in their powerful ally. He was, for instance, unsympathetic to the American hostility towards Mao's China, perhaps unwilling to recognise that the loss of China in 1949 was almost as traumatic an experience for the then Administration as was Vietnam for a later generation. Younger also took a similar view of those who advocated an aggressive policy in Iran, as is clear from the document Geoffrey Warner has here made available for the first time in the Appendix. This diary, therefore, offers not only a version of the course of international events in 1950–1, but also a contemporary dissenting voice on how they were handled.

This somewhat critical stance also extended to Younger's observations on internal Labour Party matters. Self-identified on the left of the party by his sympathies for Aneurin Bevan, Younger's entries track a growing sense of drift and disillusionment during the final months of the Attlee government. Attlee emerges as an unusually radical Prime Minister, though one who was, in Younger's view, boxed in by the caution of his Cabinet. But he was also boxed in by the uncertainties unleashed by the Cold War, prudence dictating increases in armaments and a close alignment with the Americans, notwithstanding Younger's reasoned doubts as to whether either were in fact necessary. Indeed, that Younger himself recognised this is seemingly reflected in his wry and largely accurate comment at the end of this book that the new Conservative government in 1951 would find Anglo-American relations every bit as difficult as their Labour predecessors. He was, accordingly, no more uncritical of the sometimes simplistic panaceas of the left, or of the way in which personality clashes got in the way of the formulation of policy, than he was of the actions of the Americans or of the government.

The dispassionate flavour of Younger's diaries partly derives from their method of composition. As Geoffrey Warner points out, in a sense they are not diaries at all, being written up only once every few weeks. These entries are reflective musings, rather than real-time accounts. This poses particular problems for their editor. A diary which offers a daily account can form a continuous, internally coherent narrative. One as discontinous as this requires instead that the editor must, perforce, provide linking text in order to contextualise the original account. Doing so is a delicate task. The editor must avoid being overly intrusive, whilst also striving not to go to the opposite extreme and becoming merely dull. Warner admirably succeeds in this balancing act. Younger's original entries are illuminated by appropriate commentaries and enlivened by a leavening of quotations from contemporary letters and documents, or from subsequent interviews. These very much add to the value of this text and the light it casts on the foreign-policy dilemmas of the period. Whilst the Cold War dominates the landscape, as Younger's comments show, there was nevertheless a lively internal and inter-allied debate about how that Cold War should be handled. In the critical account it offers of Anglo-American relations in a crucial period, however, it is also an important contribution to the study of alliance diplomacy, and in particular to the understanding of this significant, if often fraught, partnership.

Peter Catterall

Acknowledgements

My greatest debt is, of course, to the family of Kenneth Younger, especially to Lady Elizabeth Younger, his widow, and to Sam Younger, their son. Their generosity in giving me access to Kenneth Younger's diaries and papers and, even more perhaps, their continuing support and encouragement over the years are much appreciated. They must have wondered, as indeed did I, whether this book would ever see the light of day.

The fact that it did is mainly due to Dr Robert Mallett of the University of Birmingham, who introduced me to the original publisher, Frank Cass, now part of the Taylor & Francis group.

Many institutions and individuals have provided help in the preparation of the text, commentary and notes. Of the former, I should particularly like to thank the staffs of the National Archives in Kew, the Bodleian Library in Oxford, the Library of Nuffield College, Oxford, and the Museum of the Argyll and Sutherland Highlanders in Stirling; and of the latter, Dr Michael Hopkins of Liverpool Hope University, Mr Gordon Marsh and Mrs Jane Liddle.

In conclusion, I should like to express my gratitude to Carl Gillingham and Chris Flanagan, who performed the onerous and usually thankless tasks of copy editing the original manuscript and producing the index. Any errors which remain after their painstaking work are entirely the author's responsibility.

Geoffrey Warner, September 2004

Editorial principles

The criteria which have guided me in my selection of material from the diary were to exclude (a) almost all references to family and other personal matters and (b) constituency business; but to include everything else except where, in my view, it adds little or nothing to the historical record.

In addition to the diary, Younger kept a collection of papers, both public and private. I have made use of these in the Introduction and the main body of the text principally, but not exclusively, where they are unavailable elsewhere, for example in the National Archives, and where I consider them to be of historical interest.

Omissions in the text of both diary and papers are indicated by three dots (. . .). These can cover anything from a few words to whole paragraphs. Insertions are shown by means of square brackets [ ]. I have mostly used these for purposes of clarification – perhaps excessively – but also occasionally for correction, notably in the case of punctuation, where in the diary Younger frequently omits the second comma in a parenthesis. I have also silently corrected the occasional spelling mistake to avoid having to use (*sic*).

Younger's orthography in the diary is inconsistent but I have nevertheless followed it. Thus 'PM' is sometimes 'P.M.' and 'US' 'U.S.' Another feature is his frequent use of a squiggle instead of 'and'. I have indicated this by the use of the ampersand, &. Where the word 'and' appears in the text, Younger actually wrote it.

A consequence of following Younger's orthography is the presence of inconsistencies between his usage and that employed in the notes and commentary. An obvious example of this is in Younger's use of the Wade-Giles system for transcribing Chinese names, while the notes and commentary use the more recent and widely accepted Pinyin system.

All this may irritate the general reader, while at the same time failing to satisfy the scholar who is acquainted with even more precise conventions for editing and reproducing original manuscripts. I can only plead that I was trying to preserve authenticity without doing so to excess.

Abbreviations

DBPO – *Documents on British Policy Overseas*
Series II, Volume I. *The Schuman Plan, the Council of Europe and Western European Integration 1950–1952* (London: Her Majesty's Stationery Office, 1986).
Series II, Volume II. *The London Conferences, Anglo-American Relations and Cold War Strategy, January–June 1950* (London: Her Majesty's Stationery Office, 1987).
Series II, Volume III. *German Rearmament, September–December 1950* (London: Her Majesty's Stationery Office, 1989).
Series II, Volume IV. *Korea 1950–1951* (London: Her Majesty's Stationery Office, 1991).

FRUS – United States, Department of State, *Foreign Relations of the United States*
1950, Volume III, *Western Europe* (Washington, DC: US Government Printing Office, 1977).
1950, Volume VII, *Korea* (Washington, DC: US Government Printing Office, 1976).
1951, Volume VI, *Asia and the Pacific*, Part 1 (Washington, DC: US Government Printing Office, 1977).
1951, Volume VII, *Korea and China*, Part 1 (Washington, DC: US Government Printing Office, 1983).
1952–1954, Volume X, *Iran 1951–1954* (Washington, DC: US Government Printing Office, 1989).

H.C. Deb. – United Kingdom Parliamentary Debates ('Hansard'), House of Commons, Fifth Series.
Citations are by volume and column numbers.

NA United Kingdom official records in the National Archives, Kew.
CAB 21 Cabinet Secretariat
CAB 128 Cabinet Minutes
CAB 129 Cabinet Papers
CAB 131 Cabinet Committees

CAB 134 Cabinet Committees
DEFE 4 Chiefs of Staff Minutes
DEFE 5 Chiefs of Staff Papers
FO 371 Foreign Office General

Nuffield Transcript
Typed transcript of interview between Professor Richard Rose and Kenneth Younger, dated 27 December 1961. Copies in the Younger papers and in the Library of Nuffield College, Oxford.

N.B. All quotations from Crown Copyright documents in the National Archives or elsewhere are reproduced by kind permission of the Controller of Her Majesty's Stationery Office.

Introduction

When he was elected for the Lincolnshire fishing constituency of Grimsby in the General Election of 5 July 1945, Kenneth Gilmour Younger was just one of the 259 new Labour MPs whose election contributed to the biggest landslide in British politics since 1906 and which resulted in the formation of the first majority Labour government under the leadership of Clement Attlee. Younger's background, however, was hardly typical. Born on 15 December 1908, his family was staunchly Conservative. Indeed, his grandfather, the brewer George Younger, was made a viscount in 1922 as a reward for the important services he had rendered to the Conservative and Unionist Party after he was appointed its chairman in 1916, and his great-nephew, also named George Younger, was a Cabinet minister in Margaret Thatcher's Conservative government of the 1980s.

Following his education at Winchester and New College, Oxford, Kenneth Younger was briefly a barrister before he was recruited into the Security Service, or MI5, in 1936. The following year he joined the Labour Party. Why he made this break with family tradition is not clear, but it seems that the Spanish Civil War and the appeasement policy of the Conservative-dominated National governments of the 1930s towards the threat from Nazi Germany and Fascist Italy had something to do with it.

During the Second World War, Younger was given the rank of major. He worked in the division of MI5 which was responsible for the supervision of aliens, becoming its head in 1942. In the spring of 1943 he was the British member of an international commission which investigated political prisoners and internees in French north Africa. He was then posted to the intelligence branch of the Supreme Headquarters Allied Expeditionary Force (SHAEF), which was preparing the invasion of western Europe, and was attached to the staff of General (later Field-Marshal) Montgomery for the rest of the war. All the evidence indicates that he performed his wartime duties not merely well, but exceptionally so.[1]

By this time Younger had decided that he wished to enter politics after the war and asked for his name to be put on the Labour Party's list of parliamentary candidates. Shortly before D-day (6 June 1944) he attended a selection meeting at Peterborough along with the future Prime Minister,

Harold Wilson. Both were unsuccessful. While stationed in Brussels during the winter of 1944/5, however, his name was put forward for Grimsby. There was no one else in the field – Grimsby not being deemed a winnable seat – and he was duly selected.[2]

Following the Labour victory, Younger soon had his foot on the bottom rung of the ladder of promotion when he was appointed Parliamentary Private Secretary (PPS) to Philip Noel-Baker, the Minister of State at the Foreign Office, the post which Younger was himself to occupy five years later during the period covered by this book.[3] As PPS to Noel-Baker, Younger was given a seat on the preparatory commission for the first General Assembly of the fledgling United Nations, an organisation which was to figure prominently in his subsequent career. He also attended the first meeting of the UN Security Council in London in January 1946 and later recalled that he 'was one of the first who saw pretty clearly . . . how difficult the Russians were going to be', although he admitted that it took him 'quite a time' to realise that they were not so much difficult as impossible.[4]

Younger followed Noel-Baker to the Air Ministry in October 1946, but one year later he became a junior member of the government as the second Parliamentary Under-Secretary of State at the Home Office. This new post had been created because of the large amount of Home Office legislation which was to come before parliament and Younger helped to pilot such important measures as the Criminal Justice Act, the Representation of the People Act and the Children's Act, all of 1948, through the House of Commons.

Early in 1950, after four-and-a-half years in office and a mass of legislation which established the modern welfare state and nationalised several key industries, Attlee called a General Election. It took place on 23 February and, although Labour polled even better than it had done in 1945, its share of the vote fell slightly, while the Conservatives increased both their vote and their share of the poll, which was enough to reduce the government's overall majority in the House of Commons to a perilous five seats.

Younger held on to his constituency easily enough, but with a reduced majority. In his diary entry of 27 February 1950, he commented that Labour had done badly in the home counties and other suburban seats, which he attributed to the fact that these prosperous areas 'never really knew the slump' and could not therefore compare the present situation and its 'minor annoyances' with the serious hardship of the pre-war period. At the same time, he correctly drew attention to the effects of the redrawing of constituency boundaries, which as one historian has observed, was carried out 'with scant regard for Labour's electoral prospects'.[5]

Despite this, however, Younger thought there should be no watering down of Labour's policies to appeal to disaffected middle-class voters. On the other hand, he thought it might be possible to encourage sizeable sections of the salary-earning class, such as teachers amd civil servants, by fiscal measures which discriminated more in favour of earned as opposed to unearned income. 'I am sure,' he wrote, 'that no social revolution can have any permanence unless a new class is created which has a strong vested interest in its continuance.' The working class already had a vested interest in Labour's success. If the government could make some of the professional classes feel that their interests coincided more with those of the workers than the owners of property, Younger believed that Labour could attain sufficient momentum to sustain a further programme of socialisation and a planned economy. This was important in the international as well as the national context, for, as Younger explained, 'I think the big question of the moment is whether Britain is to continue to give a lead in social-democratic government to a world which seems to be largely slipping back to its prewar views or else, in the east, going communist.'[6]

There was an echo here of the beliefs of Labour leaders in the earlier years of the government. As Ernest Bevin put it in a paper for the Cabinet's Defence Committee on 13 March 1946, 'we are the last bastion of social democracy. It may be said that this now represents our way of life as against the red tooth and claw of American capitalism and the Communist dictatorship in Soviet Russia.'[7] Similarly, in a party political broadcast on 3 January 1948, Clement Attlee contrasted the rival ideologies of Soviet communism and American capitalism and pointed out that Britain was situated not only geographically but also philosophically between the two super powers. 'That is not to say,' he emphasised,

> that our ideas are in any sense 'watered down capitalism' or 'watered down communism'; nor that they constitute a temporary halting-place on a journey from one creed to the other. Ours is a philosophy in its own right. Our task is to work out a system of a new and challenging kind, which combines individual freedom with a planned economy, democracy with social justice.

In working out this new system, he said, the Labour government was 'giving the lead which is needed not only by this country, but by Europe . . .'[8]

Bevin had initially dreamed of creating a 'third force' in world politics, consisting of the British Commonwealth, the western European countries and their colonies, which could remain truly independent of both the Soviet Union and the United States, albeit allied to the latter. Unfortunately, important Commonwealth countries like Canada and Australia were no longer prepared to have their foreign and defence policies coordinated in London – if, indeed, they ever had been – while the western European countries insisted upon pursuing the goal of a federal 'United States of Europe', a policy which, then as now, the British government found unacceptable. A third factor which undermined Bevin's vision of a 'third force' was the onset and intensification of the Cold War in which the Soviet Union was perceived as threatening not only American but also British vital interests throughout the world. By 1949 the concept of a 'third force' had been abandoned in favour of an 'Atlantic community' in which Britain would act as a loyal number two to the United States, a concept symbolised by the formation of the North Atlantic alliance in April of that year.[9]

The Russian explosion of a nuclear device in August 1949 and the communist victory in the Chinese civil war in October only heightened Cold War tensions across the globe. It was a challenging time to be involved in the formulation of any country's foreign policy, let alone that of Britain, which still enjoyed great power status despite the relative decline in its position since the Second World War.[10] It was at this point that Kenneth Younger was plucked from the Home Office and plunged into the world of foreign affairs.

The story of the period between February 1950 and October 1951 is best told in Younger's own words and mostly from the pages of his diary. Of course Younger's diary is not, strictly speaking, a diary at all, for it was not written up on a daily basis or anything like it. Preserved for the period in question in two seven-and-a-half-by-five-inch hardback notebooks, the document takes the form of entries of varying length written every few weeks or so. Except where it is specifically stated, Younger did not add to or alter these entries subsequently. They are, therefore, a contemporary record – written 'in the midst of events' as he himself put it[11] – and their value to the historian stems from this. What the document lacks in immediacy, it more than makes up for in reflection. These are not hasty jottings, dashed off in the heat of the moment, but more considered assessments of events and personalities but without the disadvantage of the distortion which inevitably comes from hindsight.

As a junior minister in a busy department at a very busy time, Younger had, in his own words, 'far too much work and too little authority'.[12] He repeatedly refers to his intermittent involvement in various policy issues and his consequent inability to exercise much influence on decisions, but this only seems to sharpen his judgement and certainly does not detract from his powers of observation. His descriptions of ministers and officials are incisive and occasionally devastating. There can be few more convincing portraits of a once-great administration in decline than that which emerges from the pages of Kenneth Younger's diary.

The issues with which Younger had to deal as Minister of State encompassed all the major foreign-policy problems of the period: Britain's ambiguous relationship with western Europe (the Schuman Plan), the Cold War (the conflict in Korea and German rearmament) and decolonisation (the Iranian oil crisis). Connecting and decisively influencing them all was the Anglo-American 'special relationship', on the nature of which some of Younger's comments are as relevant today as when they were originally written.

After the Labour defeat in the General Election of October 1951, and despite the fact that he was a member of the Opposition front bench, Younger became progressively disillusioned with parliamentary and party politics. By 23 December 1955, following a second electoral defeat for Labour in May 1955 and the election of Gaitskell as party leader after Attlee's retirement, he was writing in his diary of his deep dislike of the House of Commons: '[M]y desire to get away from it,' he wrote, 'has been growing steadily, until I can hardly bear to be there at all.' This, he explained,

> has nothing to do with my attitude to politics as a whole. It arises from the fact that, in opposition, the pace tends to be set by cranks, exhibitionists and the very large section of members who simply enjoy the party game & make no attempt to relate what they say to what they would do if they had responsibility.[13]

The Suez crisis of 1956 briefly made him feel that he could still perform a useful function, and even Gaitskell, who clearly did not like him, paid tribute to his assistance in drafting the section on the United Nations in his speech in the debate in the House of Commons on 2 August 1956.[14] By the end of 1957, however, he began to think of leaving parliament altogether and pursuing a new career. The directorship of the Royal Institute of International Affairs (Chatham) House, of which he was vice-chairman from 1953–5 and again from 1958–9, became vacant and, after some hesitation, he accepted an invitation to apply for the post and was offered it at the end of 1958.[15] When he informed Gaitskell of his decision to leave the House of Commons at the next election, he ruefully noted in his diary that the Labour leader 'left me in no doubt at all that my going is, from his point of view, not even a minor inconvenience'.[16]

Since the Labour Party was beaten for the third time in succession at the General Election of October 1959, Younger had no reason to regret his decision. During his eleven years at Chatham House he streamlined the somewhat archaic structure of the Institute and rid it of much dead wood. Without his efforts, the RIIA would not have become the highly respected foreign policy think-tank it is today. While he was still there, he did have an opportunity to return to active politics after Labour's return to power under Harold Wilson in October 1964. Aware of the lack of government experience of many Labour MPs after thirteen years in opposition, Wilson offered Younger the post of Minister of State for Disarmament, together with a life peerage. Younger turned both down. As he explained in his diary, he did not see much scope in the job and, in any case, 'Having been the second minister in [the] F.O. in 1950–1, I was not much attracted by the 4th-ranking post in 1964!'[17]

Although the period from 1950–71 (when he retired from Chatham House) was dominated by international affairs, Younger's interests and influence ranged more widely. His liberal instincts in home affairs were demonstrated during his chairmanship of the Howard League for Penal Reform between 1960 and 1973 and it is significant that his last two major speeches in the House of Commons were on the Wolfenden report on homo-sexual law reform and the report of the committee on Obscene Publications, in both of which he argued for change.[18]

He also became one of 'the great and the good', that select body of people who tend to be called upon to serve on government committees and enquiries. Thus, he was appointed in 1970 to chair the official enquiry into privacy, the first time any government had tackled the subject, and in 1972 he served on the Diplock Commission, which examined the problems faced by the courts in Northern Ireland following the onset of the 'troubles'.

In 1974 Younger was appointed Chairman of the Lambeth, Southwark and Lewisham Area Health Authority (Teaching) following earlier experience in hospital administration as a member of the Council of St George's Hospital Medical School and as Chairman of the board of governors of St George's from 1966–9. Someone who knew him well at this time has observed that the area health authority was one of the largest in the country. Its political complexion – this period saw the emergence of the so-called 'loony left' in London – also made it hard to manage. As he had done so often in the past, Younger performed his duties with considerable skill and tact, and it is possible that, had he lived, he might have been able to prevent the subsequent financial problems encountered by the authority and the installation, for the first time in the country, of commissioners to run it.[19] Sadly, after a brief illness, Younger died suddenly on 19 May 1976. Although he never succeeded in reaching the peaks of public life, it would be a rash person who claimed that he lacked the ability to do so or that the country would not have been a better place if he had.

1   To the Foreign Office, February–August 1950

On 28 February 1950, Younger wrote in his diary:

The P.M.[1] spent yesterday and to-day in forming his government. At 3 o'clock I was sent for and told that he wants me to be Minister of State [at the Foreign Office][2] in succession to Hector McNeill who is being promoted to the Scottish Office or some other cabinet post. I hadn't expected promotion, and I hadn't really wanted it, but I can't help being gratified at having got it. I know Chuter[3] is largely responsible, as he told me had recommended me for promotion. It appears that I am also well thought of by Ernest Bevin[4] – why, is something of a mystery. It is a big promotion for me. My reaction is partly incredulity & partly nervousness. I hadn't really thought of myself as getting above the general run of parliamentary secretaries so soon. I think I have done well at the Home Office, both administratively and in the House [of Commons], but it has all been on a rather pedestrian level. Reliability rather than brilliance must certainly be what recommends me to the P.M.

I don't feel particularly exhilarated – rather the reverse. Just as, during the election, when I was being mobbed in the market & found myself thinking 'It was roses, roses all the way', so now I can't help being most impressed by the fortuitous & insubstantial nature of these political promotions. However it is a grand job, & will extend me to the full. I can only do my best & hope that things will go all right. It is not at all clear how much I will have to go abroad, but now that we have this tiny majority, I may not be able to go so much . . .

The next diary entry was on 12 March 1950, soon after the new Parliament had met.

. . . The King's speech[5] was unexciting but sensible and had nothing controversial in it. The Tories however have moved two amendments, one on housing still to come, and one last Thursday[6] demanding postponement of the Steel Act.[7] This was pressed to a division which was won by 310 to 296. Everyone on both sides who was not actually in bed ill voted!

I have listened to very little of the debate, which has consisted largely of maiden speeches. My impression is that our debates are going to be far too like an election campaign to be interesting or useful. The signs are that the Tories will concentrate on harrying the government as much as possible, but without actually trying to bring it down for a while. Our only defence must obviously be a completely firm front, with no concessions or signs of weakness. Otherwise the situation will be intolerable. We need not be provocative, but it would be fatal to let ourselves get pushed around.

... The French President's visit[8] has made it difficult to get down to solid work. We went to a reception at the French Embassy one night and to the Ballet at Covent Garden the next. Owing to the division on Steel, I only got to the latter half-way through. I also went to a lunch given by [the] F.O.[9] in the painted hall at Greenwich, where I had to receive the guests (other than the King and the President) on Ernie Bevin's behalf ... The visit as a whole was a great success. The London crowds turned out in force, the floodlighting was excellent & the weather springlike. We were told by members of the French Embassy that the President was surprised and delighted at the warmth of the welcome he got. Of course it doesn't signify much in the way of goodwill towards France. It was largely the enjoyment of a spectacle & the undoubted popularity of our own royal family. All the same it was a successful gesture.

In [the] F.O. I have been trying to get down to learning my job. It is mainly a question of reading and reading at present. I gave an official lunch[10] to Dr. Jessup, the US Envoy who was passing through on his way from S.E. Asia to Washington. A very civilised and charming man. He is really a professor but has been given the rather surprising task, in conjunction with two other academic characters, [Raymond] Fosdick & [Everett] Case of inventing a South-East Asia policy for the State Department! I can imagine many people doing the job much worse than he will, but it is no mean task to give any group of people, let alone people who are neither politicians nor regular foreign service men.[11]

The issues arising daily in [the] F.O. are vast. Obviously my only course is to try to be efficient in my daily job, but to keep my mouth shut for a while on major questions. I can see already that I am going to find my slant on many problems to be appreciably different from that of the office, but whether the difference will amount to a real divergence on policy I am not yet at all sure. My two private secretaries, Michael Hadow and [Denis] Speares both seem intelligent, lively and pleasant. I shall get on with them all right.

I need not bother to comment on the other government appointments except to note that Ernest Davies is [Parliamentary] Under Sec[retary] in [the] F.O. I think I shall get on all right with him. Poor Philip N[oel]-B[aker] has got pushed out of the Cabinet,[12] & it was only after much coming and going that he was offered Fuel & Power where he has now gone. He is of course much upset. I cannot blame the P.M. for not wanting him in the Cabinet. I myself never really want to know his views on difficult problems. There is something unreal about his whole personality and process of thought ...

The only event of political importance discussed in the next entry in the diary on 18 March 1950 concerns the so-called Seretse Khama affair. On 8 March, the British government announced that it was withholding recognition of Seretse Khama as chief of the Bamangwato tribe in the Bechuanaland Protectorate for a period of not less than five years, during which time he would not be permitted to enter Bechuanaland without special permission. This action was justified on the grounds that there was a division of opinion in his tribe concerning his right to become chief on account of his marriage to an Englishwoman, Ruth Williams, while he was a student in Britain in 1948. Some correctly alleged, however, that the British government had bowed to pressure from Rhodesia and, more especially, South Africa, where there was considerable opposition on the part of the ruling white population to mixed marriages. Younger's comment was as follows:

... I am very apprehensive of the repercussions of the government's decision upon our whole colonial policy & our reputation in India & the east. I have a feeling that there may be very large ripples from this pebble dropped in the pool. Certainly the publicity has not been successfully handled & we have a bad press from all sides. It is not impossible that the Seretse case might become a symbol of the great conflict of the age between white and coloured in Africa. If that should turn out to be so I fear that we are getting ourselves on the wrong side, albeit with fairly reputable intentions ... [13]

The next diary entry was written on Easter Saturday, 8 April 1950, at the Youngers' weekend cottage. It refers, for the first time, to an issue which was to dominate much of Younger's period at the Foreign Office: the divergent policies of Britain and the United States in the Far East.

... I badly needed a rest. I have found my new job very exhausting. It is not so much the amount of work as the fact that it is all more important & of much greater general interest than most of the Home Office work. The result is that one is much more in the limelight, and everything one says in public attracts attention & often criticism ...

In the office there is a steady flow of important issues. So far I have not had to take any major decision, though I have been nominally in charge of the office for a week or so in Ernie [Bevin]'s absence abroad.[14] The most tiresome item has been a dispute about 70 Chinese aircraft now in Hong Kong whose ownership is in dispute between the Americans and the Chinese Communists. I have had to see the [American] Ambassador Lew

Douglas twice & have been to the Cabinet on it.[15] It is just one of a number of relatively small issues which raise the question of our relations with [the] U.S. and our capacity to resist undue pressure from them. In addition this particular matter highlights the fact that we and the Americans are running two inconsistent policies towards the Far East. I anticipate a great deal of friction in the coming months.

This divergence between British and American policies towards the Far East stemmed from the differing evaluations by London and Washington of the Chinese communist regime which had come to power in October 1949. Although it realised that the latter's ideological stance would not predispose them towards cooperation with the west, the British government regarded the Chinese communists as an independent political force with considerable popular support. It therefore extended diplomatic recognition to the Chinese People's Republic on 6 January 1950. The US government, on the other hand, regarded Mao Zedong and his followers as unrepresentative tools of the Soviet Union and therefore refused to recognise the new regime.

In his diary entry for 8 April 1950, Younger goes on to discuss Ernest Bevin and his relations with the Americans. He also describes the first full-length foreign affairs debate of the new Parliament and gives a characteristically frank evaluation of his own performance. The entry also sees the emergence of another theme which was increasingly to trouble Younger during the months that followed: Bevin's deteriorating health and the serious effect which it had upon the conduct of British foreign policy.

My impression is that Ernie Bevin stands up to the Americans well when he himself is convinced of what the right line is. Where he appears to be weak, e.g. in Germany, the reason is that he is already half in agreement with them anyway, rather than that he can't withstand pressure.

There has been one full dress foreign affairs debate in the House [of Commons].[16] It came too early from my point of view, and so far as I was concerned it was a flop. What happened was that the Opposition chose the debate & then tried to make Ernie open it. He refused & said he was going to wind up. The result was that [Winston] Churchill[17] opened, and I was deputed to follow after allowing a Liberal to speak between me & Churchill. Of course no one ever knows what Churchill is going to do on such an occasion. He might make a broad statesmanlike speech or he might merely do some electioneering. Anyway I felt that it would hardly be my job to speak directly in reply to him. That seemed more a matter for Ernie to deal with in his winding up. Moreover, Ernie was so unwell in the few days before the debate that I had no proper chance of talking to him, and I had little idea of how his mind was working on the main problems of the moment. I therefore felt that the only thing I could do was to make my own speech, without too much regard to what Churchill might say.

I was a bit dismayed on getting the various briefs from the office. There was really nothing of much interest in them. Certainly there was no 'message' of any kind that the office wanted to put across. Strang[18] told me that the most useful thing would be to make a self-contained statement of our policy of economic and political co-operation in Europe & the east. He said, rightly[,] that Ernie had never done it.

Anyway that was what I attempted, and so far as it went my speech wasn't too bad. The trouble was that it didn't go far, and didn't really say anything of interest on the main topic which, as it turned out, formed the central theme of the debate – Germany.

Winston [Churchill] made a very lofty speech on Europe & Germany. It was well done as a dramatic performance, & the whole House & the press hailed it as one of his great speeches.[19] I suppose that I must have been too preoccupied to listen closely, as I was quite unimpressed and did not feel that he had said anything significant at all. All he did was to talk in an emotional and romantic way of 'France & Britain holding out their hands to Germany.' He did not mention any of the difficulties or resolve anyone's doubts. I was frankly astonished when I found what an impression he had made. On re-reading his speech I have not changed my mind.

When he had finished the House emptied and only a few came back when I rose to follow the Liberal. I felt from the start that my speech was bound to be a failure from a parliamentary point of view. For one thing the whole debate was at its flattest moment, & for another the House was obviously intending to spend the day speculating about Germany, German rearmament etc. On this I had almost nothing to say. What I had to say, though useful as a statement in Hansard, was almost a total loss as a contribution to the debate. And that is how it turned out.[20]

In the circumstances I doubt if I could have done anything else, with the Foreign Secretary due to wind up later on. It was disappointing to have a failure in one's first debate – and very irritating to be told by Eden[21] in his closing speech that I had merely strung together a number of clichés – this from Eden of all people! It wasn't a fair criticism, but what would have been fair, would have been to say that it was a dull statement which did not help the House in making up its mind on any of the major problems under discussion.

Ernie was so ill that day that he spent most of it in bed. He staggered in late to hear Churchill & then again later to hear Eden. No one felt sure that he would get through his speech. However, he rose unsteadily, & said a number of very sound things, speaking in a low weak voice. He succeeded in making Churchill very embarrassed over the rearming of [the] western Germans, & he said some things which gave encouragement to the French. Unfortunately he also said some things which will discourage progressive forces in Germany, especially the Social Democrats, and he again gave a rather unfortunate impression of continued hostility to Israel and undue respect for the Arab states in the Middle East. On balance, however, he did fairly well.[22]

The next day he went off to abroad to meetings in Strasbourg & Paris,[23] where he seems to have been in much better health, & to have done well. At close quarters I find him in many ways impressive. He has a firm grip on realities in most respects, and an ability to make up his mind. All the same, I cannot see how anyone of his age[24] & his state of health can decently go on very much longer as Foreign Secretary. In many ways he has done a fine job, but I doubt if he has much more to contribute now. We need someone younger who is looking twenty years ahead rather than two. I have a feeling that he may not stay very long after May, when he has a series of high-level talks with Acheson[25] and Schuman[26] in London.[27] No doubt much will depend on the date of the election. If there were to be an election in June, there would be no changes before that, but if this parliament lasts until October, it may be that something will have to be done beforehand.

I do not feel very optimistic about the possibility of my making any significant contribution to policy in the short time that I am likely to hold this job. It will take me some time to get my own ideas sorted out and to establish myself with Ernie and with the office. Only when I have done that will there be much point in trying to exert any influence. Of course, if there were a change of Foreign Secretary there might be more scope for me to make suggestions – at any rate if by any chance the new S[ecretary] o[f] S[tate] was Hartley,[28] which is by no means impossible.

Younger also recorded an interesting conversation with Aneurin Bevan, the Minister of Health and stormy petrel of the Labour government, whose views on foreign affairs and defence were to diverge increasingly from those of most of his Cabinet colleagues during the months that followed.

Nye Bevan said to me the other night that he thought Foreign Policy might play quite a big part in the next election. He thinks the country passionately wants some new initiative to be made for an agreement with the Soviet Union. I think this is so, but at the moment I can see no basis for thinking that the Soviet Union is thinking in terms of genuine agreement. Nye rather disputes this. He feels the Soviet empire is already overstretched and would be glad of a détente. I am inclined to think, on the other hand, that their successes in Asia,[29] combined with a reasonable belief that we are likely to have great trouble over German and Japanese competition & that our own unemployment position may soon become much more serious will be sufficient to make the Russians stonewall at least for a while longer. I do not think they are yet willing to do anything which would help 'the west' to solve its economic problems or to reduce its military commitments.

This appears to be Acheson's view. I don't yet know what Ernie really thinks on the subject.

The next entry in the diary is not until 14 May 1950. The reason was pressure of work.

In the last month since I made an entry in this diary I have been busier than ever before in my life. It has been [an] interesting and valuable experience, but rather more than I can manage & I hope it doesn't last. Not only is it too tiring, but it prevents one ever reading the press properly or talking to one's friends or fellow members [of Parliament]. Already I feel out of touch with everything but the F.O. which is thoroughly bad for my judgement.

The main reason for all this is that Ernie Bevin went straight into hospital and and has only just come out in time to do the talks with the French & Americans which have been on all this week.[30] In consequence I was nominally 'in charge of the office' & had to keep going to Cabinet & various committees & deal with a mass of things which normally I should scarcely see.

To begin with I had to go to Brussels for a weekend on April 15th. For the Consultative Council of the Brussels Treaty.[31] Shinwell[32] headed the delegation and Gaitskell[33] went for the Treasury. I had nothing to do in the conference but listen, and I had of course some responsibility for watching the F.O. angle on defence matters. I found it all rather boring, & not a great deal got done. There was as usual too much entertainment & one had no spare time. George Rendel our Ambassador [in Brussels] & I went to a couple of meals there as well as to a Belgian Banquet.

The French delegation was good & I was glad to get a chance to meet [Robert] Schuman who is Foreign Minister and [René] Pleven who is defence. Schuman is a very attractive person, and politically good in many ways. I would not however pin much faith to him as he is an odd personality with too much of the mystic for my liking. A bachelor & a very devout Catholic who is said to be very much under the influence of the priests.

I also liked the Dutch Foreign Minister Stikker,[34] but the Belgians were intolerable. They are in a dynastic crisis over Leopold & have no mind of their own.[35] Quite apart from that they are a most disagreeable bunch headed by van Zeeland[36] & an appalling creature called Devèze.[37] On their form at this conference they might as well be written off as allies.

On return to London I was launched into a mass of Cabinet meetings dealing with very diverse subjects – Far East, Middle East & many other topics. One day[38] I had to make a statement in the House [of Commons] announcing our recognition, simultaneously, of the union of Jordan and Arab Palestine, and of the gov[ernmen]t and state of Israel. It was the first popular government statement on Palestine since the war so I got a bit of unearned credit for it! . . . [39]

We have just finished a week of high-level talks – 2 days with the Americans, and 3 days with the Americans & French. The coming week there will be a meeting of the Atlantic Council.[40] Ernie Bevin came out of hospital just in time to do them, but still very far from well. There were 14 days of preliminary official discussions, and of course a lot of inter-ministerial argument in preparation for the meeting of ministers. During all of this Ernie was bedridden, not fully able to cope, but sufficiently available to prevent anyone from taking his place.[41]

At the talks themselves he has been far from his best form. He said himself that he is 'only half alive.' The doctors give him so many drugs that he often had difficulty in staying awake and in taking a proper grip of the meetings, of which he has been chairman. At other times he has been quite all right, and in fact very good.

Personally I think it is something of a scandal that the P.M. has allowed the situation to develop. These talks have been heralded as 'the most important since the war', but in fact they have been very largely futile, and Ernie's condition has been a big contributory factor. The fortnight of official talks seems to have been mainly occupied in platitudes. Anyway it resulted in the presentation to ministers of a series of anodyne documents which, in my view, quite failed to point up the things which really require discussion.

Things might have been saved if Dean Acheson had come over with any clear idea of what he wanted to say, but in the event he failed to take any lead at all. There were two days of 'bi-partite' talks[42] which, I had understood, were to be the most intimate and important. I attended three out of the four meetings and have seldom been more embarrassed. Ernie was too ill to speak at two of them & could barely read out the agenda, let alone take charge. Acheson, when the ball was thrown to him, looked vague & harassed, said a few banalities and stopped before one thought he had begun. Ernie then said to his advisers 'What's the next item?', and on we went. This happened on numerous occasions. Once Makins[43] had to butt in from the second row to prevent the whole meeting from collapsing for want of direction. Even on the item which was supposed to be the vital one – Germany – Acheson had nothing to say & frantically appealed to McCloy,[44] his High Commissioner[,] to help him out. McCloy, obviously taken by surprise[,] improvised a few rather inconclusive thoughts to which our High Commissioner, Brian Robertson,[45] replied, and once more on we went.

After that particular meeting I was only narrowly dissuaded from going to the P.M. and telling him that he really must come & preside & send Ernie back to bed.[46] The main reason why I didn't do this was that the P.M. was seeing Ernie morning & evening every day & it seemed an impertinence not to leave it to him. Moreover, as Acheson was equally futile, even a vigorous chairman could not have produced any result. On one afternoon we got a measure of progress on a middle eastern question. Otherwise the 'bipartite talks' passed away as though they had never been.

Apart from Ernie's health the causes of the fiasco were, I think, that Acheson's nerve has been broken by the vicious campaign against him in [the] USA, so that he dares not put forward a constructive policy.[47] I also think the F.O. & State Department officials must be blamed for letting a conference of this kind meet with such ill defined objectives. The whole thing has been rather shocking to me. I have enough experience not to take a romantic view of what statesmen can achieve when they meet, but I wouldn't have believed that anything of this level of inanity could occur if I had not been present to see it.

Neither the available British nor American records of these conversations[48] convey the atmosphere of chaos and futility so vividly described by Younger, which only goes to show the limitations of official records. Thus, in his memoirs, Dean Acheson wrote, 'I found Ernest Bevin in distressing shape when we met him and his staff ... He had recently undergone a painful operation and was taking sedative drugs that made him doze off, sometimes quite soundly, during the discussion. His staff seemed accustomed to it, though I found it disconcerting. At any rate, our talks got nowhere . . .'[49]

Perhaps it was Acheson's disconcertion rather than his domestic political difficulties which accounted for his own indifferent performance at the talks, a possibility which Younger conceded in 1976 after re-reading his diary in the light of Acheson's comments.[50]

As already indicated, one of the issues which Younger felt had been inadequately dealt with during the Anglo-American talks was policy towards the Far East. On 11 May 1950, he wrote the following minute on the subject to Bevin:

I am worried that there seems to have been so little clarification of the Far Eastern question in the course of the Bipartite Talks. I had understood that the long and short-term implications of the divergent policies of the U.S. and U.K. were to have been thrashed out, but as far as I can gather there seems to have been a minimum of discussion ending merely in an agreement to disagree. Presumably that means that for the next few months at least we are to pursue our present policy with the object of 'keeping the door open' in China without paying too much attention to American susceptibilities, while they will feel free to carry on their relations with the Nationalists in Formosa without much regard to its effect on our position.

It seems to me that there is a danger that in this way we will get the worse of both worlds.

It seems clear that in the short run we are not going to get much change out of the Peking Government. British interests in China are likely to have a very thin time and we will probably not get an exchange of Ambassadors. The decision over the Chinese aircraft in Hong Kong[51] and the decision not to allow Chinese Consuls to go to Malaya,[52] both of which seem to me to be correct decisions, will no doubt be used by the Peking Government as an excuse for prolonged stone-walling. Nevertheless, it seems to me far too early to assume that Peking will not eventually want relations with us and will not be prepared to do trade with us, and I think we should therefore do everything that is practicable to improve our relations. Almost the only thing we can do in this way at the present moment is to assist the Chinese in the United Nations, a point to which they apparently attach importance, and I am not myself satisfied that our policy of abstention is the right one.[53] It is possible to justify it on rather technical grounds where subordinate bodies are concerned, but I find it very hard to justify when it comes to any of the senior organs .... I cannot myself see what we gain by refusing to vote for the Peking Government. It does not appear to give us any bargaining lever with them. It seems to be little more than an attempt to ride two horses at once.

I would hope that before Mr. Acheson leaves we could take some opportunity of impressing upon him our view that the People's Government should be accepted in the United Nations. From the general point of view of the functioning and prestige of the United Nations it will be damaging if the Russians boycott the Security Council and the General Assembly in September.[54] Quite apart from this I feel that our weak position in Hong Kong gives us a very real motive for wanting to see the People's Government inside the United Nations. A new government like the People's Government is likely to attach great importance to its position as the one permanent Asian member of the Council, and it seems to me a good deal less likely that they will allow themselves to be used by the Russians for a direct or indirect attack on Hong Kong if by so doing they endanger their position in the United Nations. Such a situation is unlikely to arise this year but might well arise fairly quickly once they have settled with Formosa.

I realise that the American difficulty about altering their policy in China arises almost wholly from domestic political causes and from the coming elections.[55] No doubt we must accept it as a fact that Mr. Acheson cannot do much till the elections are over. That, however, seems to me no reason why we should not present our own policy to him much more fully than seems to have been done in the Bipartite Talks.[56]

In a minute on a Foreign Office copy of this document Bevin wrote, 'I will talk to Acheson', but in a further minute on 31 May 1950 Michael Hadow, one of Younger's private secretaries, noted that he had been unable to do so. British policy was changed so that the British representative could vote in favour of Chinese communist membership of the United Nations Economic and Social Council, but by the time the issue came up at the United Nations on 3 July 1950, the Korean War had broken out and the matter was deferred.[57]

Younger's diary entry for 14 May 1950 continues:

The 'tripartite' talks with Acheson and Schuman,[58] though not of much significance, were less deplorable than the 'bipartite'. Ernie was pretty sick at the morning meetings but quite lively each afternoon. At least the meeting went forward competently from one item to the next, and there was usually some exchange of views & some clarification of the respective positions. I cannot honestly say that any disagreement which existed at the beginning had been resolved at the end, or that anything had been achieved which could not have been better done through the 'usual channels'.

The impressions which I derived from this series of talks were, (1) that the Americans are under a compulsion to 'hot up the cold war' in every way on account of the state of American opinion, while the French, for a similar domestic reason[,] are above all anxious not to seem to close the door against agreement with the Russians. The difference is only one of emphasis but it is important. (2) We & the Americans want to start building up an Atlantic Community which includes and transcends Western Europe, while the French still hanker after a European solution in which the only American function is to produce military & other aid. This difference is important because it stems from two quite different conceptions. Ernie has no faith in the solidity or efficiency of France or Belgium & believes W[estern] Europe will be a broken reed, and will not even attract the loyalty of Europeans or impress the Russians unless it is very solidly linked to North America. I think this is realistic though depressing.

Here Younger highlights what is still the principal dilemma of British foreign policy: the choice between a pro-American and a pro-European orientation. Successive British governments have tried to avoid making a choice, even denying that one is necessary, but there is no doubt that the dominant tendency has been to lean towards the United States. Even as Younger was putting pen to paper, the dilemma presented itself in a particularly acute form. The diary entry for 14 May 1950 concludes:

The major event of the week occurred the day before the tripartite talks began when [Robert] Schuman announced in Paris his government's plan for merging the French & German coal iron & steel industries under a single authority.[59] The details and implications of the scheme are still quite vague. Neither we nor the U.S. gov[ernmen]t were consulted or informed,[60] the object being to achieve a big psychological jolt. This was achieved.

Officially we have welcomed the idea, & so have the Americans. So has Adenauer[61] for the German Federal Republic. Indeed it seems clear that he *was* in the know.[62] Privately we all have doubts & misgivings. In view of the political complexion of French & German gov[ernmen]ts & their links with heavy industry, one cannot but expect that this will develop along old fashioned cartel lines. It need not do so, however, and if we can get the scheme executed in a way which safeguards the public interest and limits the power of the vested interests in the international authority, then it *may* be a step forward. On the other hand it may be just a step in the consolidation of the catholic 'black international' which I have always thought to be a big driving force behind the Council of Europe.[63]

If the scheme goes through, we will clearly have to be associated with it in some way. At present it is hard to see how we can actually join it. It is however too soon to make up one's mind. The French themselves have clearly not thought the scheme out, let alone explained it to anyone else.

The real architect of the Schuman Plan was not the French foreign minister, but the head of the French economic planning commission, Jean Monnet. Schuman's role lay in assuming the political responsibility for accepting Monnet's proposal and for steering it through a French cabinet which was taken as much by surprise as the rest of the world. Monnet's motives appear to have been, at one and the same time, to limit the threat posed by great power competition for the allegiance of the German Federal Republic, to allay French fears of German industrial and political domination, to bring the Federal Republic into the comity of European democracies on a more or less equal footing and, finally, to lay the foundations for a federal union of Western Europe.[64]

The next entry in Younger's diary is dated 20 May 1950 and deals with the meeting of the Council of the North Atlantic Treaty in London from 15 to 18 May.

... It was not exciting, but it was quite efficient and it registered all the decisions which it was intended to register. These included (a) a statement of policy towards Germany, which went some way beyond the Petersberg agreement;[65] (b) the setting up of a small permanent body of deputies within the Atlantic Organisation. This is an important practical step towards getting on with the practical aspects of defence. There was also useful discussion about the future economic organisation of W[estern] Europe. This will only become urgent when Marshall Aid ends in 1952, at which time [the] OEEC will either pack up or take on new form. This problem raises the issue to which I referred two pages back[66] regarding 'W[estern] Europe or an Atlantic community.' The French again directed most of their efforts to limiting the Atlantic idea. There was no decision, quite rightly. There are nearly 2 years in which to decide, & the general trend of public feeling will obviously change a good deal in the meantime.

Ernie Bevin seemed a bit better this week, and got through successfully to the end. It would be untrue to say that he did as well as he would have done if fit. I thought that he was very much in the hands of the officials, and did not really seem to be fully on top of the job. However he did as well as was necessary, in view of the disappointing attitude of the Americans. Acheson got a little better as things went on (he was in the chair) but he really had no contribution to make, and I doubt if anyone could have made much progress with him on the subjects that really need thrashing out, such as the Far East, Germany and economic relations.

I did virtually nothing in these talks, though I had to speak once or twice on small points in Ernie's absence. I was fairly busy with other things ...

Bevin's health dominated the next entry in Younger's diary, which was written on 29 May 1950.

I had a very busy week before the House [of Commons] rose on Friday[67] for the Whitsun recess. Ernie Bevin was in the office all the week, but has now retired again for at least a month. He is to have another slight operation, and even if all goes wholly according to plan he will need a prolonged rest. The total absence cannot be less than 6 weeks, & I shall be surprised if he is really back at work [in] under two months.[68] If anything goes at all wrong, I imagine he will have to retire, but he said to me 'I will resign if I do wrong, but not for ill health. That's right isn't it?' I couldn't bring myself to say it was! I think, and have already written once before,[69] that it is already rather a disgrace to have allowed our foreign policy to be run so long by a man who is not in a fit state to do a full job. I think it probable that opportunities of all kinds have been missed all along the way. He just manages to get through his essential work, but he has no energy left for anything more.

I have to admit that when he pulls himself together he usually does pretty well for short periods. In Cabinet (which I have been attending with him recently) he appears to be asleep, but then suddenly weighs in with comments which show that he knows exactly what has been said. One can't help admiring his guts & nervous energy. At the same time it is rather pathetic, for there is no doubt that he is in considerable pain & is only a shadow of his real self. I think what carries him on is his stupendous egotism. He really believes himself to be wholly indispensable.

I don't suppose the PM would let him stay if this parliament was likely to last long, but I dare say he would prefer not to have to make a change until after a general election. Such a course is just excusable if the election is not later than October, but only just excusable ...

It looks as if I shall have a pretty hectic time after the holiday. I am in charge of the office 'with access to the P.M.', which in effect means that I have to run the whole thing unless major policy issues arise. It is a considerable opportunity, though rather a strain while it lasts ...

Unfortunately for Younger, two 'major policy issues' did arise while he was in charge at the Foreign Office: the British reaction to the Schuman Plan and the outbreak of the Korean War. His next diary entry, on 12 June 1950, deals with the first.

... Just at the moment when parliament rose and Ministers scattered, there began a rapid exchange of notes from London & Paris with a view to calling a conference to work out the [Schuman] plan. Ernie B[evin] was in hospital, the PM and Cripps[70] in France, Ernest Davies in Geneva & most of the rest of the Cabinet out of London, so I found myself nominally in charge of the proceedings with only occasional reference to Herbert Morrison[71] who was acting for the P.M. In fact of course the officials had the bit very much between their teeth. Every move was discussed between Sir E[dward] Bridges,[72] Plowden,[73] Strang & Makins, and by the time I had a hand in it it had become pretty hard to make much impact. There was also a slightly lower level official committee permanently sitting and trying to work out a British version of the plan.[74]

The issue, at this stage, was fairly simple. The French proposed calling a conference and invited all participants to subscribe *in advance* to a short communiqué embodying (a) pooling of [coal] iron and steel industries under (b) a high international authority whose decisions should bind governments [and] (c) a treaty to be signed *as a first step* accepting (a) & (b) before the practical implications were discussed.

The object of this very rigid attitude apparently was to bind the Germans & prevent them from subsequently putting forward conditions; it was also designed to prevent us or anyone else from going back on the idea of a binding international authority & reverting to the OEEC conception of control by a committee of ministers.

I was very much impressed throughout with the importance of trying to make some scheme work, & consequently of finding some basis upon which we could participate from the start. In this I was virtually alone. Strang said frankly that he thought the whole thing nonsense & was a French attempt to evade realities. Makins, though less hostile, felt that we should not get committed, that the Franco-German talks would inevitably break down sooner or later, and that we would then have a chance of coming in as deus ex machina with a solution of our own. In addition, Makins was the main protagonist of the view that the plan is largely designed to get away from the 'Atlantic' conception and to revert to a 'European-third-force-neutral between [the] USSR & [the] USA'. I have no doubt that there is some force in this view. Quite certainly that is the notion of one big group of Frenchmen & possibly also of the Germans.

Anyway, one rather anxious day in which I was arguing for acceptance of the French formula with a reservation, in order to get in on the talks, it became clear that we should have to refuse the prior commitment & let them go ahead without us if they must. This is what happened. Herbert Morrison & I went to see Ernie Bevin in hospital & get his view which was of the simple 'I won't be dictated to' variety! Then a skeleton cabinet meeting endorsed that view, we had one try at getting the French to call a preliminary meeting of ministers, they rejected the idea & that was that.

The Younger Papers and other sources enable us to flesh out this account of a decision which was to have such important consequences for Britain's future relations with western Europe. On the evening of 1 June 1950, the French government sent what was in effect an ultimatum to the British government, demanding that the latter accept, within the next twenty-four hours, the terms of a communiqué which would commit Britain to place its coal, iron and steel industries under a supra-national authority, or the other interested governments would proceed without it.[75]

Herbert Morrison's biographers, relying in this instance upon an interview with Younger, described what happened next. 'Younger went in search of Morrison,' they wrote, 'accompanied by Edwin Plowden ... They finally tracked him down, eating in the Ivy restaurant after an evening at the theatre, and called him into a side corridor to point out the need for an urgent decision. Morrison thought a while and then shook his head. "It's no good," he said, "we cannot do it, the Durham miners won't wear it." '[76]

Clearly unhappy at this instant reaction, Younger drafted a note for Morrison's consideration early the following morning, 2 June 1950, in which, although endeavouring to present a balanced view of the risks involved in accepting or rejecting the French ultimatum, he made it clear that he was more impressed by the dangers of staying out of the negotiations on the Schuman Plan than those of going in. The note, which is in the Younger Papers, reads as follows:

1 The French have stated that if we cannot accept their latest proposal by 8 p.m. tonight, they must proceed without us. While this may be bluff, we must assume as a possibility that the decision about British participation will have to be taken by that time.

2 In addition to the intrinsic difficulty of deciding what Britain should do, we have the further practical complication that acceptance of the French proposal appears to go beyond what the E.P.C. envisaged,[77] and that many members of the Cabinet are not available to consider the new situation. However this may be, it would not be justifiable to treat it as decisive. It would be wrong to imagine that the choice lies between taking a risk by accepting the French text or playing safe by rejecting it. The risks involved in the latter case are certainly no less than in the former ...

3 While we may during the day succeed in agreeing upon a modified formula, or even on postponing the issue, you may think it wise to make preparations to hold a meeting of available ministers in case a final decision has to be made. If you so decidė I will have sets of relevant documents (texts, telegrams etc.) made ready for use at the meeting.

Risks involved in accepting the French formula for participation.

1 The full Cabinet may later cause difficulties on the ground that the formula goes beyond ministers' expressed intentions.

2 Public opinion in the U.K. may understand the formula as a commitment to surrender sovereignty, even though, on a strict interpretation of the text, it does not go as far as this.

3 When negotiations start, the French may seek to treat the formula as a commitment to sign a treaty incorporating the surrender of sovereignty. If we refuse to accept this, we will be accused of bad faith. (Provided

that we make the proposed reservation I do not think that this charge could be sustained.)

4 Starting from acceptance of this formula, we might get manoeuvred into a position where withdrawal was so awkward politically that we would be under great pressure to accept an unpalatable scheme against our better judgement.

Risks involved in rejecting the French formula for participation.

A On the assumption that the other countries would reach agreement without us.

5 We should be seriously criticised in Europe and the U.S.A. for rejecting the first imaginative proposal put forward for rationalising a key portion of European heavy industry and for making Western Germany a good member of the 'Western Club'.

6 On the economic side our coal and steel experts view with some alarm the consequences of our having to compete with a powerful, integrated group of European industries formed without our participation.

7 While we might be able to join in the plan before it reached finality, we should, by failing to participate at the start, greatly reduce our chances of getting a scheme worked out on lines proposed by ourselves. (In this connection it is relevant to note that the official working party appears to be making fair progress and may well be able, within the next week to produce an outline scheme which would safeguard British interests. In this we are almost certainly ahead of all other countries.)

B On the assumption that the other countries would fail to reach agreement without us (or would even decline to proceed with the negotiations).

8 The French would be seriously humiliated at the failure of their much-applauded initiative and would feel very bitterly towards us. The consequences to Schuman are hard to calculate but would surely be serious.

9 The only gesture of friendship made by France to Germany would have been frustrated by us, and the difficulty of finding any way of reconciling German revival with the French demand for security would be greatly increased. The French feeling of inferiority and isolation, which makes them so hard to deal with, would be enhanced.

10 While West Germany's reactions can only be guessed at, she would be bound to feel grave doubts about the sincerity of the west in professing to want to see her reinstated as an equal, though with guarantees against renewed aggression. In particular she would be more than ever convinced that British policy was dominated by fear of commercial competition and not by security considerations. This might have grave consequences as she becomes more nearly independent of the occupying powers and has to make her choice between an eastern and western orientation.

11 A possible way of using German resources (and eventually manpower) in the defence of the west would be thrown away.

12 One possible sequel to the failure of the Schuman plan is the linking on a purely industrial basis of the French and German industries, along the lines familiar before the war.[78]

According to a later minute to Sir William Strang, Younger explained that he had not shown the above document to Morrison as he had originally intended because his intention had been overtaken by the visit which he and Morrison had paid to Bevin in hospital and by the subsequent Cabinet meeting. He added, however, that he had made the points in his note orally in the conversation with Bevin and Morrison.[79]

While the official record of that conversation does not confirm this,[80] another version of the same conversation, given by Bevin to the journalist Leslie Hunter, shows that Younger did indeed fight his corner. 'Morrison and Younger,' wrote Hunter,

... went round to Bevin's bedside to discuss the problem. Bevin, always keen to bring on the younger ministers, turned to Younger and asked, 'Well, young man, what do you think of it all?' Younger was all for Britain joining in. Bevin listened attentively and then heaved a sigh. 'Splash about, young man, you'll learn to swim in time,' he commented and then turning to Morrison began, 'Now, Erbert –' and got down to the details of how to keep out of this embarrassing offer.[81]

When asked about this story by Richard Rose in 1961, Younger replied:

I've been asked about this before and I can't remember having known of that remark, but it would be absolutely in keeping.[82]

The Cabinet meeting mentioned by Younger took place on the evening of 2 June 1950. Morrison presided, there were seven other Cabinet Ministers present, plus Younger and a junior Treasury minister. The meeting approved a reply to the French ultimatum proposed by Bevin, which rejected the French formula for participation in the Schuman Plan conference and suggested a meeting of ministers to discuss the issue.[83] The French government rejected this counter-proposal on the following day.

Younger's diary entry of 12 June 1950 continues:

On reflection I think we really had no choice & that seems to be the almost unanimous view of the press. Nevertheless it is unfortunate that we appear to be 'out on a limb' as usual, and no doubt we shall come in for a good many kicks as a result. What is more important is that no one has yet produced either a coherent explanation of how the French plan can be made to work, or any alternative proposal for eventually bringing Germany safely into the community of W[estern] Europe & the Atlantic. That major problem is still quite unsolved, & this French initiative, even if it was a bit haywire, offered & perhaps still offers a possible solution if only we can get it on a workable basis.

Among all the numerous uncertainties is the uncertainty about the ideological implications of this type of plan. It could easily be a purely capitalist cartel with U.S. backing. In view of the reactionary character of nearly all the governments concerned (and their strong Roman Catholic complexion) it would be surprising if there were not an element of this in the conception. Moreover the most vocal support is from thoroughgoing reactionaries like Reynaud,[84] and on the German side there is even said to be a link up with Moral Rearmament and Dr. Buchman.[85] If this is so, it seems to be an argument for coming into the negotiations early & preventing the development at the start. If we do not, the probability is that there will be an industrial get-together anyway.

I have as yet no clear view of what we ought to do next. The French conference meets in ten days, and it is unlikely that we will do anything before then except pursue our own efforts to produce a workable scheme.

During all this there has of course been a lot of comment about my being in nominal control, with most of the Cabinet away, when such a big issue was in the balance. On the whole the comment has not been unfair, & it has certainly given me a bit of useful publicity . . .

The Schuman Plan also figures prominently in the next diary entry, dated 6 July 1950, although it had already begun to be eclipsed by the Korean War.

These last three weeks have been even more hectic than usual. Not only has the follow-up on the Schuman plan, including a two day debate in the House [of Commons], been giving us all a great deal of work, but right in the middle of it (the day before the debate, 25th June) a North Korean army invaded South Korea,[86] and set in motion a whole train of action of which the consequences are still largely guesswork. For us this meant an immense amount of to-ing & fro-ing between Ernie [Bevin] (still in the London Clinic) and the P.M., and attendance at Cabinet & Defence Committees. I didn't speak in the House either on Schuman or on Korea, but I had more than enough without that . . .

About [the] Schuman plan there is relatively little to say. The Paris Conference has been going on without us, but there was a longish adjournment & they haven't got very far. There is a draft French plan which uncompromisingly insists upon a supra-national authority, with very little democratic control. We could not possibly accept that. The nations at Paris[87] have not rejected it, but most have expressed misgivings, except the Germans, who have everything to gain by acceptance of the scheme, with a good prospect of dominating it before long.

In the meantime we have worked out a scheme of our own, based upon intergovernmental cooperation, which is really quite constructive.[88] If the

French negotiations break down, our plan may serve to rescue something from the debris. It is however at least as likely that something on supranational lines may be agreed upon by the other powers, and that we may have to fix up some association with it. Our experts seem quite happy about either solution. From the political point of view, i.e. from the point of view of Franco-German relations, the second might perhaps be the better.

The debate,[89] in which the P.M. and Stafford Cripps spoke for the government, was not exciting. I gather Winston [Churchill] thought he might be able to cause a split in our ranks and beat us on it, but instead there was a very small split in his own, & we got through quite comfortably, with the outside public taking really very little interest in it all. The main subject of Tory criticism was not government policy, but a pamphlet issued by the National Executive of the Labour Party on European Unity, which appeared on the very day when the P.M. announced in the House why we could not at present take part in the plan.[90] The timing of the publication was fortuitous, & its tone was a good deal stiffer than government statements had been. It had been written not in connection with the Schuman plan at all, but as a brief for Strasbourg,[91] and its object was to show why we could not join a purely W[estern] European federation. On the whole the pamphlet is good, but unfortunately it was ineptly launched by Hugh Dalton[92] at a press conference when he was so rude to all the foreign journalists that they went away determined to make trouble for him. They picked out odd sentences from the text & gave the impression that the Labour Party would cooperate only with socialist governments in Europe – a line which at the present moment would cut us off from everyone outside Scandinavia! All this caused a bit of party bickering which is not yet dead owing to a rather silly speech by John Strachey in which he, in effect, attacks the Schuman plan as a reactionary plot designed to prevent the public control of European industries.[93]

The Korean situation has now knocked Schuman right into the background of public consciousness. It is a fortnight since the invasion, and we are only at the very beginning of what promises to be a difficult business.

Over 40 nations have now weighed in behind the U[nited] N[ations] in approving resistance to the aggression. US troops are however still thin on the ground [in Korea][94] & are having a bad time and are retreating. They may need considerable forces to restore the position, but they can scarcely afford to fail now & everyone seems convinced that the thing will have to be seen through.

The real question is how it is to be localised. The collective effort is being made solely in relation to Korea & solely in support of a U[nited] N[ations] resolution,[95] but the Americans have also taken steps to prevent the Chinese communists from capturing Formosa, the last foothold of Chiang Kai-Shek.[96] If the quarrel were to spread to Formosa, that would at once bring in

China, and would antagonise nations like India & Pakistan who would never support an American war against an Asian power.

In his interview with Richard Rose in 1961, Younger recalled how he had taken the draft US statement of 27 June to Ernest Bevin in the London Clinic. The Foreign Secretary, he said,

put his finger on the Formosa part and said, "Why did they have to do that? Before we know where we are we'll all be in a world war for the sake of Chiang Kai-Shek. This was not necessary. It has nothing to do with Korea. Why can't they keep it to Korea?"[97]

Younger's diary entry for 6 July 1950 continues:

It looks as though the divergence between US & British policies in the Far East ... must now become acute. Even if the Soviets do not want to turn this incident into a major conflict – & I should be surprised if they do – they have a good chance of using it either to drive a wedge between [the] US & [the] UK, or else to force [the] UK into open hostility with the new China. I foresee a very difficult period in our dealings with [the] USA. I think we could get agreement with Dean Acheson & the State Department, but US policy is now so largely under military influence that I am most apprehensive about the quality of US statesmanship in this sphere.

These events have naturally increased the tempo of my work even further. Ernie Bevin, however, is doing a good deal, though still in the nursing home, & much of the top level work is done between him & the P.M. In the debate in the House [of Commons][98] the PM opened & Herbert Morrison wound up. They would have done better to let me speak, for Herbert made an awful mess of it. It didn't matter much, as there was virtually no disagreement on policy.

The outbreak of the Korean War focused attention even more closely upon the need for defence against possible communist attack. Did the Korean War signal a new readiness on the part of the Soviet Union and its allies to resort to armed force in pursuit of their objectives, as President Truman had claimed in his statement of 27 June 1950? Were the west's defences adequate to meet the challenge? If not, how could they be made so without undermining the west's standard of living, which was one of its chief assets in the struggle against communism? More particularly, would it prove necessary to rearm the old enemy, Germany? Younger tackled these problems in a perceptive minute to Bevin on 6 July 1950. I have been unable to trace a copy at the National Archives.

The following points have occurred to me on reading various documents relating to Western European defence ...

1 The present Western defence budgets are clearly inadequate if we are to reach our targets for 1954 or 1957. The deficiencies are large and increasing, and it seems clear that only a major alteration of priorities as between 'guns and butter' could fill the gap.

2 Such a change of policy would be politically difficult. I do not think it would be impossible if the public could be convinced that its result would be adequate defence, but as far as I can see this would be very far from the case. A defence of Western Europe based mainly upon France and Britain would be very shaky even if the targets were reached. Account must be taken of French morale, particularly civilian morale. It seems very unlikely that this would be anything like as good as it was in 1940 when it is recognised to have been pretty poor.

3 If, therefore, we are planning for a defence against a full-scale Russian attack, it seems clear that we must be able to count upon a large and immediate contribution from the United States or Germany or both. As regards the United States, it does not seem likely that she will commit large land forces to be available immediately upon the outbreak of war in Europe. In this connection the Far Eastern position is relevant, since it appears that present policy is to keep Japan wholly disarmed, a course which will presumably commit the United States to having considerable forces of her own available in that theatre. As regards Germany, great as the political difficulties are, her rearmament seems essential if Western defence is to be real. In the first place it might then be possible to defend the Elbe instead of the Rhine, with great effect upon the morale of the Low Countries and France. In the second place it would make available efficient manpower on a significant scale. It is at this point that the Schuman Plan becomes relevant. If the Plan were to succeed, French fears of German rearmament might be overcome, and later Germany might be brought into the Atlantic Pact. If the Schuman Plan failed German rearmament could only be carried out at the cost of a serious diminution of French willingness to play her part in Western defence. The Chiefs of Staff seem to accept German rearmament as essential but think it is still too delicate a subject to be broached. However this may be, it is surely essential to face the fact that, without the Germans, realistic Western defence by 1954 or probably 1957 is out of the question.

4 The decision whether the disagreeable course of immediate German rearmament has to be accepted obviously involves a choice between two estimates of future Soviet policy. If we believe, as many military authorities here and in the United States seem to believe, that the Russians are likely to engage in large-scale military aggression as soon as they are strong enough to do so, then we must face German rearmament and German dominance in Western Europe. Such a course will probably put paid to any real democratisation of Western Germany since it will put the nationalists and militarists back in the saddle. A further logical consequence of this view is that we should give up hope of increased

East/West trade and go along with the Americans in imposing what are virtually economic sanctions against the Soviet bloc.

5 These unhappy consequences can be avoided only if we deliberately decide to take a different view of future Soviet policy, i.e. if we assume that while there may be a prolonged period of cold war and while the Soviet Union may promote various minor adventures on the Korean model, she is very unlikely to invite a major clash with a great power and in particular is very unlikely to try and sweep over Western Europe. On this assumption our logical policy would be to give up for the time being an attempt at full-scale Western defence, and to assume that we need only maintain sufficient forces in Western Europe to deter the Russians from attempting an almost bloodless walk-over. On this assumption we could allow ourselves time to fight the Communist Fifth Column in France and Italy[99] by economic and social methods. The German political problem would have to be solved by a combination of East/West trade, contribution to development of backward territories and emigration. On this basis, while some German military contribution to the West would have to be envisaged in due course, there would be no immense urgency about it.

6 At present we do not seem to be clearly following either of these policies. We appear rather to be purporting to build up a military defence capable of resisting a full-scale attack within the next few years, but without German participation. We are not succeeding in doing this and all our military advisers know it. Military advisers are stressing the need for much larger defence expenditure, but their plans carry no conviction because everyone can see the grave social and political consequences of larger defence budgets, while no one believes that by that means alone any effective defence will be achieved ... [100]

On 22 July 1950, the United States government informed fellow-members of the North Atlantic alliance of its own plans for an increased defence effort and asked them to provide, by 5 August, the 'firmest possible statement ... of [the] nature and extent of increased effort, in terms of increases in both forces and military production, they propose to undertake'.[101]

The Chancellor of the Exchequer, Sir Stafford Cripps, tabled the British government's proposed reply for discussion by the Cabinet on 1 August. Existing plans involved defence expenditure totalling £2,590 million over the three years 1951/2–1953/4, and Cripps proposed to increase this to £3,400 million. In view of what happened in the following year,[102] it is interesting to note that the main objection to these proposals came from Aneurin Bevan. The government's policy, Bevan told his colleagues

> had hitherto been based on the view that the best method of defence
> against Russian imperialism was to improve the social and economic

conditions of the countries threatened by communist encroachment. The United States Government seemed now to be abandoning this social and political defence in favour of a military defence. He believed that this policy was misjudged, and that we would be ill-advised to follow it.

Other ministers disagreed, however, and the Chancellor's proposals were adopted.[103]

It will be noted that Bevan's argument picked up on some of the points made by Younger in his minute of 6 July 1950 printed above and since we know from a later passage in the diary that Younger was in touch with Bevan during this period,[104] it is tempting to speculate whether the junior minister had any influence upon the Cabinet Minister's views. There is, however, no evidence that Bevan saw Younger's minute or even discussed its contents with him. Younger was himself present at the Cabinet meeting of 1 August 1950, but is not recorded as having intervened in the discussion.

Four days later, on 5 August 1950, Younger reflected upon the continuing crisis in Korea (where the British government had reluctantly agreed on 25 July to commit ground troops), the differences between British and American policy, and the possible consequences of increased rearmament. He concludes with a critical assessment of the senior members of the Attlee government whom he had seen close-up during the period in which Bevin was in hospital.

Parliament rose a week ago.[105] Ernie Bevin is due back in the office on Monday[106] and I am due to leave for three weeks' holiday on the same day. I am hoping not to have to put my feet inside the office from now to 1st September.

That probably ends the long period during which I have in effect been continuously 'in charge of the office', and as continuously overworked. It has been a great experience and on the whole I have come through it with reasonable credit. I do not think I have made many glaring mistakes and I think I have taken as much of the burden off Ernie [Bevin] and the P.M. as was practicable. Obviously with matters like Korea & the Schuman Plan, many of the decisions could only be taken by senior ministers acting together if not by the whole cabinet. I am not able to sway the cabinet as Ernie might, & I would have been wrong to try. All I could do was to know my stuff, put my points clearly & persistently & rely on the P.M. to handle the Cabinet if necessary. In point of fact there has been surprisingly little disagreement over most of the issues of recent weeks ...

I shall not trouble to write much about the substance of the work I have been doing. Much of it has related to Korea, which is a matter of history. With most of the decisions being taken in Washington, & with the Security Council sitting in New York [,] there has been a daily rush to clear and send out urgent instructions almost every day. Often we have had to face situations caused by the ham-handedness & excitability of the Americans who are, understandably, in an emotional and difficult state. At the present time they are engaged in a desperate effort to stabilise a front which is little more than a bridgehead around Pusan.[107] It is not sure that they will succeed and their prestige is of course very much involved. In consequence they are not inclined to pay much attention to the longer-term issues arising from their lack of policy in the Far East, and we are fighting a constant battle to prevent them from deliberately courting trouble with China, over Formosa and other matters.

Underneath what often seem petty disagreements and misunderstandings there is I think an important difference of viewpoint between us. The Americans, with only a few exceptions[,] seem to have decided that a war with 'the communists' is virtually inevitable & likely to occur relatively soon, say within 3–5 years. They regard all communists alike, no matter what their nationality[,] and assume that they are all dancing to Moscow's tune & are bound to do so in future. It follows from this that the main problem is how to win the war when it comes, & there is no room for any subtleties in dealing with the Chinese. They are enemies & must be recognised as such.

We on the other hand, despite growing pessimism, still give first place to the effort to prevent war. We do not accept it as inevitable, & we are therefore unwilling to prepare uninhibitedly for an early war if by so doing we make war more likely or seriously impair our ability to raise our own & other living standards over a longer period of years.

I do not suppose the Americans would admit to the point of view I have mentioned. They may not even be conscious of it. But most of their soldiers act on it & it is only upon that assumption that US political behaviour makes any sense at all. This applies particularly in their attitude to China. They are simply not interested in our view that China, if properly handled, could in the long run be separated from Moscow. Because such a development does not seem likely to happen quickly, the Americans discount it. There will, they argue, be a war anyway before anything useful can happen.

All this is very dangerous. We now have the two great powers both apparently believing, for different reasons, that a major war is bound to come, & that in itself makes war much more likely.

When I left the office today William Strang said 'I do not suppose things will have changed much by the time you get back.' I can certainly see no prospect of a change for the better. The most likely changes, if there are any at all, would be the defeat of the Americans in Korea & their complete evacuation (which is still a possibility) and a Chinese attempt to take Formosa, which the Americans would resist. Either of these events would lead to a serious deterioration of the whole Far Eastern position.

I made a vain attempt to get the Cabinet to discuss the consequences of a US–Chinese clash over Formosa, but Ernie wouldn't have it. He was afraid of some decision which might tie his hands when the time came.[108] My view is that by backing the Americans we would endanger everything that we have achieved in Asia by our forward policy in India, Burma etc. and that we might split the Commonwealth irretrievably into white and coloured.[109] All the same, refusal to back the Americans would be a great shock to the worldwide alliance, the Atlantic Pact and the collective effort against Soviet communism. Faced with the choice, my own very reluctant view is that we would have to go with the Americans. Either way the prospects for world peace, let alone progress, would be immensely bleak.

Younger's 'very reluctant view' found support from none other than Aneurin Bevan, whom he consulted while the subject was under discussion in the Foreign Office. In a note written some time in 1954 and inserted into the diary, Younger wrote:

... He [Bevan] unhesitatingly advised that, if the clash came, we could do nothing but support the Americans. 'When you are in a world-wide alliance, you can't retreat from it on a single issue.'
During the interview, when complaining of Attlee's inadequate handling of the world situation, he used the striking phrase: 'He treats it like a piece of fretwork, when it is really a passion play.' ...

The original diary entry of 5 August resumes thus:

Already unpleasant results of this are making themselves felt in the shape of increased arms production, and the prospect of having to renounce further progress on the economic & social front for some years. Such a situation may well put an end to social democratic parties in the west, including even the Labour Party. If our main effort is to be military, and everything else becomes almost stagnant, it is hard to see how our policy can differ from the Tories['] except perhaps in ensuring somewhat greater equality of sacrifice. Moreover rearmament & large armed forces arouse enthusiasm among the Tories and nothing but despondency among us and our supporters. It is doubtful whether we can in such circumstances maintain national leadership for more than a limited period. If things get worse, coalition will loom up, official Labour & the Tories will get identified, and the communists and fellow travellers will get a big chance to take over the leadership of the opposition. I cannot foresee what I might do in such circumstances. I might easily find a coalition policy impossible, but whether I should find any more acceptable political resting place I do not know. I have a feeling that I should be obliged to rethink my basic position all over again in terms of the new situation.
I do not find much comfort in most of my colleagues on such subjects. Very few of them are, I think, interested in first principles at all. Their approach is pragmatic, and anyway they are mostly too busy to go in for

political philosophy or ideological thinking. I have been too busy myself in recent months. Nye Bevan is, of course, an exception. I usually agree with him in Cabinet, though he occasionally goes off on a wild tangent. His position is none too strong just now & he is not a member of the inner circle who really decide things. If therefore there should be any spiritual crisis within the [Labour] movement or the government, Nye would probably take a line of his own and I should be very tempted to follow him.

I admire both the P.M. and Cripps in their different ways. Intellectually Cripps is really remarkable, & Attlee certainly has an authority which would surprise outside observers. It is true that he does not frame policy personally. He leaves that to Cripps, Morrison & Bevin. He is however a very good coordinator & executive, and his detachment from personal relationships makes him quite formidable within his well recognised limitations.

I can't say the rest of the Cabinet impresses me much. As a body the Cabinet shows little cohesion or basis of common thinking. Many members would be at least as happy in a Tory government, and happiest of all in a coalition. The younger members – Harold Wilson,[110] Hector McNeil[111] & Patrick Gordon Walker[112] – are very competent in their jobs, but politically I don't warm to any of them. The two latter are too obviously on the make. It appears that they have been grooming themselves to succeed Ernie if he has to pack up! It looks as though he will disappoint them for a while at least.

Equally Herbert Morrison is waiting impatiently for Clem Attlee to go. At present I think he would be bound to succeed to [the] leadership, but I should be very sorry to see him there. He is a very astute politician but in my view lacks real stature. Although in many ways he is far abler than Clem, I do not think he has as broad or as elevated a conception of national & world affairs as Clem. As P.M. I believe he might let us down badly . . .

During the rest of August, Younger went on a well-earned holiday to France with his wife and elder daughter. Several pages of the diary are allocated to this holiday, but there is only one passage of political interest, dated 20 August 1950.

. . . I read one French paper a day – just enough to be sure that Bevin was not dead and that no new war was breaking out! The news is pretty depressing. Korea is a very tough affair, & obviously cannot be put right quickly or without great effort. As a result all the western powers are stepping up their defence budgets & there is an atmosphere of pre-war anxiety. While an early war is on the whole not expected, there seems now to be a general belief that war will come – or at least that only major rearmament can prevent it – an idea that has not noticeably helped to prevent war in the past. I think politics will be pretty gloomy when I get back . . .

2 The United Nations, September–December 1950

Although Younger returned from his holiday on 28 August 1950, the first entry in his diary after his return was not until 17 September. The first sentence explains why.

These last three weeks have, contrary to my hopes, been almost as hectic as the summer months. Ernie Bevin was only there for a week, & I had little chance to see him. Then he went off to the Tripartite meeting in New York,[1] and I was again in charge. Despite the [parliamentary] recess there has been a mass of cabinet & committee meetings, with much F.O. business, and during this last week Parliament has been in emergency session to debate defence.[2] ... Now we are in for two contentious debates on exports of strategic materials and on the nationalisation of steel. The latter might, in the present state of the casualty & absentee lists, bring the government down, which would mean an October election. It is anyone's guess; my guess is that we will scrape through.[3] Then – if we succeed – I am off to the General Assembly [of the United Nations] in New York, & may not get back much before Xmas – an awful thought.

Recently, the main interest, & most of my work[,] has centred round rearmament and especially the vexed question of a German contribution to western defence. The Americans are rushing things, too fast for the French & Germans, & possibly, even, too fast for British opinion. We are trying to stall them, but they have the bit between their teeth & I fear there will be no holding them for more than a month or two at most.

We have already referred to the acceleration of the rearmament programme.[4] As far as a German contribution to western defence was concerned, the British Chiefs-of-Staff stated unambiguously on 30 August 1950 that they saw 'no way to provide the forces needed to defend the territories of the North Atlantic Treaty Powers without German assistance'. They accordingly proposed the formation over the next five years of a West German army of twenty divisions (plus another ten in reserve), an air force of 2,100 aircraft, and some naval forces to boot.[5] This was far too much for the government to swallow, however, and the most that it was willing to accept was Bevin's counter-proposal of a 100,000-strong gendarmerie (plus another 3,000 in West Berlin) in order to match the paramilitary *Bereitschaften* which the Russians had set up in East Germany.[6]

When Bevin arrived in New York, however, he discovered that this was not enough to satisfy the Americans. They not only wanted the formation of German regular military units, but also made it quite clear that unless their allies accepted this, even if only in principle, they would not be willing to reinforce their own forces in western Europe.[7] Faced with this pressure, the British Cabinet registered its 'general agreement to an acceptance in principle of German participation in western defence' on 15 September 1950, although it is clear, even from the typically circumspect minutes, that there was a great deal of opposition.[8]

Younger had been present at the Cabinet meeting of 1 August 1950 at which the accelerated rearmament programme was approved,[9] and it was he who steered the acceptance of a German contribution to western defence through the Cabinet on 15 September. He was well acquainted, therefore, with both issues and the dangers they represented. His diary entry of 17 September 1950 continues:

The defence programme itself has not of course been my direct responsibility, but I have had, & continue to have, doubts & anxiety about its overall purpose & the appropriate scale of it. At present we are committing ourselves to a pretty heavy & growing burden, but without going far enough to give much prospect of a successful defence of the Rhine – let alone the Elbe. That, of course, is why the US are pressing for German forces; while the French are opposing because they fear it would mean that the Germans would get priority in US equipment, or would at least compete. That seems almost inevitable. The point on which I cannot clearly make up my mind is whether moderate rearmament, not amounting to adequate defence against an all out Soviet invasion of the west, is likely to be (a) merely a useless provocation & a burden on our economy, or (b) a deterrent to the Russians in any further adventures, whether large or small scale, which they may contemplate. I think the official view favours (b) and moreover envisages the possibility of stepping things up to total defence if the prospect of a world war becomes imminent. The Americans, on the other hand, want us to go all out now, at almost any expense to our living standards and without regard to the danger of actually precipitating a war by this means. Neither official nor unofficial opinion here accepts this. Like everyone else in the European theatre, we *must* work to *prevent* war, not merely to win it. I think the Americans have virtually given up hope of preventing war at all. That certainly is true of most of the soldiers, who are running a most dangerous policy.

In the meantime the Korean war seems at last to be turning in our favour.[10] There is talk of a finish in two months or so if no Soviet or Chinese aid is given to the northerners. I hope it will be so, though what the political solutions thereafter can be, baffles me at present almost completely.

The scene as a whole is most depressing. One feels one is being swept on a tide upon whose direction one has no influence at all. If war does come one will find oneself linked to allies at home & abroad with whose objectives one has scarcely anything in common, & one will have the gravest misgivings about the sort of world which is likely to emerge even from a victory. All that will be far worse than last time. I suppose it is the same sort of hollow feeling inside which so many right wing conservatives felt as they saw Hitler's war approaching. This time it is the left & the progressives who have misgivings, for they have spent so many years trying to believe the best of [the] USSR & her system, and now find that the threat to their own national interest is compelling them into reluctant hostility not only to Russia but to communist movements everywhere. All of us would leap at any chance of avoiding a conflict of this kind, even at the expense of compromise. For Tories on the other hand no compromise is thinkable, any more than the left could compromise with the Nazis in 1938.

Reflections of this kind make me dread these coming months in New York where I expect to be fighting a battle for which I have no stomach at all . . .

Younger flew to New York on 20 September 1950 to take over the leadership of the British delegation at the fifth session of the United Nations General Assembly. His first major task was to introduce an important resolution on Korea. He tells the story in the next entry in his diary, which is dated 15 October 1950.

. . . We piloted the resolution through successfully & got a good many commendations . . . I think we kept all our co-sponsors[11] (and the Americans) happy & got as good a result as could be hoped. Whether it will have any effect in Korea is of course *quite* another question. The fighting does not yet seem to be over, & the job of getting a settlement will be formidable. Throughout the whole affair one of our main objects was to keep the Indians with us. In this we narrowly failed, because our resolution contained the implication that UN troops might cross the 38th parallel into North Korea. This was unavoidable if we were ever to get all Korea united. The Indians feared however that it would bring China into the war. The rest of us thought it would not. So far it looks as if we would be proved right.

This item was a great start for me, and helped to put me on the map here. I made several speeches, all quite short & unspectacular but I think businesslike.[12] To judge from private comments, this has been thought to be a welcome change from Hector's[13] polemics. V[y]shinsky[14] was on the whole mild by his previous standards. Of course he opposed us, but he does not so far seem anxious to make a big thing of it. My view is that the Russians know that Korea has been a setback for them; but they think [the] USA & all of us will make a mess of the settlement & that within a quite short time Korea will fall into their lap once more. They therefore dissociate themselves wholly from our solution, & just wait. I think that is sound policy, & I am not at all confident that it will not succeed. I am not optimistic about the future of a 'democratic' Korea under US or UN auspices ...

Younger was right not to be optimistic about the future of Korea, but this was not so much because of the United States' or the United Nations' inability to democratise the reunified country, as of the entry of the Chinese People's Republic into the war on the North Korean side, which prevented reunification from taking place at all.

Once the Americans, the British and the other members of the United Nations agreed to defend South Korea against the North Korean attack, they were faced with a dilemma: whether to fight simply for a restoration of the status quo or to attempt to reunify the country. They chose the latter. As Attlee explained to the British Cabinet on 26 September 1950, the UN General Assembly

> ought now to consider the situation which might arise in the near future if the North Korean armed forces were virtually destroyed and North Korea was left in a state of chaos. It would be the duty of the United Nations to restore peace and order in the country as a whole, and to establish an independent Democratic Government for the whole of Korea.

This was the purpose of the resolution which Younger introduced in the General Assembly's First Committee on 30 September 1950 and which was passed, by a large majority, in the full Assembly on 7 October 1950.

In his presentation to the Cabinet, Attlee added that '[i]t might well be necessary for United Nations forces to enter North Korea for the purpose of achieving these objectives'. Indeed, it was pointed out in discussion that if UN forces did not cross the 38th parallel, 'Russia might occupy North Korea or anarchy might ensue' and that, in either case, the preservation of a stable regime in South Korea would be impossible. There was, therefore, 'general agreement that military operations could not be stopped at the 38th Parallel'.[15]

This was a truly fateful decision. The Chinese communist regime had always feared that it might be drawn into the Korean conflict, but following the Inchon landings, the headlong retreat of the North Korean forces and the recapture of Seoul on 29 September 1950, it began suggesting, both in public and in private, that its troops would enter the war if UN forces, and particularly their majority American component, crossed the 38th parallel. These warnings were largely ignored or treated as bluff,[16] but on 8 October 1950, the day after the passage of the British-sponsored resolution in the General Assembly and the crossing of the 38th parallel by US troops, Mao Zedong issued the order committing Chinese 'volunteers' to the Korean War.

It is true that the implementation of the order was temporarily stayed on 12 October as a result of Stalin's refusal to provide logistical support and air cover for the Chinese forces, but the following day the Chinese Communist Party's Politburo decided to go ahead regardless. The destruction of North Korea and an American presence so close to China's industrialised north-east was understandably seen by the regime as an unacceptable threat to its security. On 19 October 1950 260,000 Chinese soldiers began pouring across the Yalu River, the boundary between China and North Korea. On the same day Pyongyang, the North Korean capital, fell to South Korean forces.

Although the first Chinese prisoners were captured in Korea on 25 October 1950 and the first limited Chinese offensive was launched on the 26th, the full extent of China's intervention was not appreciated at first as the Americans and their allies pressed on towards the Yalu. Younger does not even mention it in the next entry in his diary, which is dated 29 October 1950.

... The Korean debate [in the General Assembly] was followed by a U.S. resolution, described as 'United Action for Peace', which was, in essence, an attempt to ensure that if another aggression occurs, the General Assembly will be able to meet & express the UN view & make recommendations, even if the Security Council is bogged down by the failure of the great powers to agree[17] & also that there will be more widespread sharing of the burden of resisting aggression. It was a rather ticklish issue, as none of us wanted to transgress the [UN] Charter or to give the Russians an excuse to walk out of [the] UN on the ground that we had proposed to amend the Charter and abolish the veto by a mere Assembly resolution.

Quite a few delegations were nervous about this. The Americans, who felt the need for the resolution owing to their own public opinion (which naturally feels that [the] US is shouldering too big a share of the Korean burden) looked like running their heads into a lot of opposition, & our job was mainly to act as middlemen, persuading them to water down their proposals in a way which would ensure a good solid vote.

John Foster Dulles[18] handled it for them. I did the main job for [the] UK with Frank Soskice[19] handling the legal questions. Dulles did it very well & was very supple in meeting most of our points. In the end he was rewarded by getting a vote [in the First Committee] of 50 for his resolution,[20] which still contained most of the things he really wanted. The main points were (1) The Gen[eral] Assembly to meet in emergency session on [the] request of any 7 members of [the] Security Council, & to make recommendations to members on methods to meet an aggression, *'including the use of armed force'*. (2) A peace observation Committee to be available to be sent on request to danger spots, to observe & report (3) a Collective Measures committee to receive reports from members as to forces they can make available in emergency to the U.N. & to study any other methods of collective security. (4) a panel of military experts to be available to advise member states on training & equipment of these forces.

The Russian group opposed, but nowhere looked like trying to make it a breaking point. They contend, of course, that the whole thing is illegal. Their case is arguable on a strict legal view, but it is certainly not conclusive, & most of us, even legalistic people like Zafrullah Khan,[21] felt that there was quite enough doubt to justify the stretching of the interpretation of the text in a way which so obviously met the needs of the organisation.

I spoke twice (& may still have to speak again in Plenary) & my speeches were well received. I myself thought them both competent, & rather liked the second one.[22]

The same [agenda] item contained a number of other resolutions, Soviet & other, whose object was to promote various types of great power talks. In the end we steered it all satisfactorily into a harmless channel and there was a unanimous vote on it – a fact which of course indicates pretty plainly that it hasn't very many teeth in it!

During this period I made a number of outside speeches which have taken up a good deal of energy. I spoke twice in UN week in New Jersey, at Montclair & at Newark.[23] Then I spoke on 'Our relations present & future with the communist world' to a dinner of New York state editors. I had what seemed to me a rather extra good short speech, somewhat theoretical &, as it turned out, a bit above their heads. I invited discussion & got none, which rather depressed me, but I have since been assured that it went well.[24]

Then I addressed a dinner of the Council on Foreign Relations on 'British Policy in Asia'. This was supposed to be, & indeed was, an intelligent and influential audience. I got a really disgracefully small amount of assistance from the office & wrote the whole thing entirely myself (indeed all my speeches have been entirely my own so far). My main objects were to make clear our case on China, and to try to explain the Indian attitude which has been subject to a good deal of rather bitter comment here. I tried to stress that Asians have quite a different view of communism from Americans or even Europeans; and that China is[,] to many of them, more important than Russia.

It seemed to go down quite well, though I didn't pull my punches on US policy in the Far East. I got virtually no criticism of my arguments. The comment was mostly rather jocular & intended to indicate that the real reasons for US policy are internal political ones. It was a good evening & I enjoyed myself.

Since the issue which Younger addressed in this speech was the one which gave rise to more discord between the United States and Britain than any other in this period, and since, despite the lack of any briefing from the Foreign Office, the speech provided such an excellent exposition of the British attitude, it is worth quoting at length.

... There is ... a certain divergence in our judgement of the best methods to pursue in winning the Asian peoples on to our side in this struggle [against communism]; and this divergence in turn is, I think, due to our different appreciation of the attitude to Communism of the Asian peoples themselves. They are inclined to fear – and Western spokesmen only too often give them cause for it – that proposals for aid from the West are prompted only by the strategic need to stop the march of Communism, and that the intention is to line up Asian countries on the side of the West in a coming test of strength with the Communist world.

In most of Asia Communism is not a bogey-man with which to scare bad children, as it is in some circles in the West. Indeed, in some areas Communism has identified itself with much-needed agrarian reform and offers to landless peasants more hope than was held out to them by previous rulers. It is therefore small wonder if events in China, though recognised everywhere to be of world-shaking significance, seem to many Asians, in the present phase, to be a fairly natural and wholly indigenous development of the Chinese revolution which has been going on for many years, and of Chinese emancipation from Western commercial influence.

This attitude to Communism in China, so different from the attitude of much of the West, is of great significance in the thinking of India and South-East Asia. All through South-East Asia there are very large Chinese populations permanently living in Malaya, Thailand or Indo-China, yet still strongly attached to China, no matter what its Government for the time being may be. It is not upon the basis of blind hostility to a Communist China that the cooperation of these widely scattered millions can be won for the West.

Nor can the cooperation of India with the West be secured upon that basis. The somewhat equivocal attitude of India in the United Nations and elsewhere, which has aroused some bitter comment in the United States, is not, I think, due to any tendency to appease Soviet imperialism, but to the predominant position occupied in Indian thinking by the problem of her relations with China rather than with Russia.

China is, after all, one of the two greatest Asian powers and, at a time when Indians are looking forward to the emergence of Asia into a position of increased influence in world affairs, it is bound to be a prime object of their policy to ensure that the Asian continent is not immediately split by a conflict between them.

That China now has a Communist Government obviously complicates the task, but Indians believe sufficiently in the essentially Asian character of China to be sceptical of her remaining for long under Soviet influence; and they believe that the best way to prevent China from being added to the already formidable forces of Soviet expansionism is to ensure that she enjoys her appropriate status in international organs, and that she has other means of contacting the world than through Soviet intermediaries.

In this Britain largely shares the Indian view. We are not ready to assume that China, which has defied or absorbed so many invaders in the past, can be easily assimilated into the Soviet system or that she will readily yield the leadership of Asia to the Politburo in Moscow. Traditional Chinese xenophobia, as well as Mao Tse-tung's personal history, suggests the very opposite. Moreover, Russian and Chinese interests in the Far East have not been identical in the past and there is no reason to believe that they are identical now. Indeed, their views may well differ on the future of Korea in which it seems that Russia and China have nothing in common except their anxiety to prevent the United States from establishing themselves permanently in the peninsula.

In view of all these factors it seems to us that the one way to force China into permanent adherence to the Soviet Union would be to ostracise her and to leave her no friend in the world but the Kremlin.

May I reinforce this argument by an illustration?

It is surely pertinent to ask oneself whether Yugoslavia could have broken with Moscow,[25] if she had had no hope of friendly association with the West and had not been a member of the United Nations.

In any case, it seems to us in Britain that acknowledged facts are a firmer basis for policy than wishful thinking; and two facts seem to us to be firmly established.

Firstly, that the Central People's Government of Peking controls the Chinese state machine, embracing all the Chinese mainland; and secondly, that ultimately any settlement of the Far Eastern area must at best be extremely precarious if China is excluded from it.

It is therefore no more than simple realism to try to live on friendly terms, and to cooperate in solving problems, with the only Government capable of speaking for China. That in our efforts to do this we have so far met with a disappointing response, and that our sincerity appears to be unjustifiably suspect in Peking is a ground for regret, but it does not change the facts, and it will not therefore change our readiness to deal with the Peking Government or our efforts to bring that Government into the United Nations ... [26]

In private Younger's view of India was more critical than it was in this speech. While he sympathised with Prime Minister Jawaharlal Nehru's policy, he wrote later in his diary entry of 29 October 1950:

... I think his judgement is erring on the side of negativeness & wishful thinking, both as regards China & as regards [the] USSR. I do my best to stand up for the Indian line whenever I can, because I think India is immensely important in the whole Asian development, & because I respect their motives for their present policy even when I think it ill-judged.

In continuation of the diary entry of 29 October 1950 on page 38 above, Younger wrote:

During this last week we have moved on to a Soviet item, which comes up in one form or another every year. It is known as [the] Resolution on the threat of a new war & consists of (a) condemnation of propaganda for a new war (b) abolition of atomic bombs[27] (c) $\frac{1}{3}$ disarmament all round and (d) a peace pact of the Big Five.[28]

It is purely a propaganda exercise and is linked with the current peace campaign which is being run by Communist parties all over the world. Consequently we all have to make propaganda replies, designed to show up the half-truths, evasions and dishonesties which lie behind the Soviet resolution. I had been a bit afraid of this item, because I have always in the past argued against the virulent anti-Soviet slanging match on which Chris Mayhew[29] and Hector McNeil engaged on this item in previous years.

Once again I made entirely my own speech, dealing with the main points made by V[y]shinsky & ending with a combined attack & appeal to the Russians, showing how un-socialist has been their post-war record in international cooperation and assuring them of the support of socialists just as soon as they really carry out a democratic & socialist policy.[30]

I felt the speech was good, and it has, on the whole, gone down well here. I haven't yet got much indication of British reactions beyond a favourable report in the Times.[31] My intuition was to strike a socialist note and to find something more acceptable to the labour movement in [the] UK & Europe than the mere vituperation of some other delegations (& to some extent of ours in past years).

Having made my main speech, I hope not to have to take part again on this item. The Netherlands, led by Dr. van Hoeven Goedhardt[,][32] are promoting a resolution in reply to the Soviet one & we are supporting it. They are doing it exceedingly well, & it is a pleasure to work with them.[33]

So far I am well pleased with my own work and that of the delegation. Comments all round seem to be favourable and *so far* we have got away without any gaffes! The next really tricky period will come when the Formosa issue crops up. We cannot discover what US policy is on this, & we look like being in a difficult position in steering a middle course between [the] US & the Peking gov[ernmen]t, who are going to be represented at the Assembly when these items come up.

One of the most wearing features to date has been the unending stream of official entertainment. Often for 10 days on end I have not had a lunch or dinner free, & there are nearly always receptions too. Generally one has to go to them, & generally they are rather dull, rather lengthy, & compel one to do one's work late at night.

Very few are worth any comment. Truman came to speak on UN day[34] & I, as one of the hon[orary] vice-presidents[,] went to the lunch given by Entezam,[35] the president of the Assembly, and Trygve Lie.[36] I got a good impression of Truman's personality. Very easy & friendly & unassuming. No special indications of culture or intellectual force, but also none of vulgarity or stupidity ...

By the time of the next diary entry, which was written on 5 November 1950, Younger was becoming both increasingly weary of life at the United Nations and concerned about developments in the Far East.

I have had nothing very exacting to do during this last week. Most of it has been occupied with a Plenary meeting at which I have had to make two short routine speeches, one on 'Uniting for Peace'[37] and one on the extension of Lie as Secretary-General.[38] The latter item is an unfortunate affair in which the Russians have tried to get Lie out because of his vigorous action over Korea. A subsidiary objection was a speech he made in Norway saying that he thought the Atlantic Pact legitimate. Most of us were not enthusiastic about Lie, who is neither strong nor very efficient, but the whole thing soon got turned into an issue of principle – is [the] U.N. going to support its chief official when he is attacked for having done his duty & has thereby offended one of the powers which wields the veto? The Americans got very steamed up about it, and the old idiot Austin[39] even threatened (quite unnecessarily) to veto any candidate other than Lie. Meanwhile the Russians, having made no response to our attempted consultations over many weeks, began to propose a whole series of semi-suitable candidates from Latin America, India, [the] Philippines etc. whom they would never have considered for a moment in any other circumstances. All failed to get the necessary votes in the [Security] Council, or else withdrew their candidatures, & eventually Lie's term was extended for three y[ea]rs by the Assembly, with the Russians threatening not to 'recognise' him. It is all very unfortunate & may lead to much bickering & inconvenience, if it suits the Russians to make it a pretext for causing inconvenience. Some of us had misgivings about forcing upon the minority a Sec[retary]-Gen[eral] whom they distrust; but, as so often happens, the Russians have led the affair in such a way as to make it impossible for anyone to meet them.[40]

I am feeling rather flat and bored, possibly because I am not for the moment keyed up with speeches or difficult decisions. I wish it was all going to be over soon, & I could get back to see Betty & Susie & Lucy,[41] but I'm afraid that is certainly more than a month ahead.

I have a feeling that the Assembly, which seems to be losing impetus now in its 8th week, may soon enter a new phase. The U.S. mid-term elections occur on Tuesday Nov[ember] 7th, & one can never tell what difference that may make to the US attitude on some questions. It might also influence the Russians, if, as many think, they are anxious to start consultations on a number of problems. Until the elections are over they would not think it much use taking an initiative, since 'sound anti-communism' seems to be essential here for all vote-catching U.S. politicians. If the Democrats were to do well on Tuesday, the Russians might then think an approach useful. (Such an approach might have either of two objects – a genuine desire for settlement or a merely tactical desire to take the edge off

American keenness to rearm. I am bound to say that, in my judgement[,] the second is the more likely.)

Then there are very worrying new developments in China, which might give the conference a new twist. It is now clear that there is some Chinese intervention in Korea, though it is still uncertain how far this will go;[42] and it is also clear that the Chinese are overrunning Tibet, by a combination of military invasion & internal coup d'état.[43] The second of these events is important mainly as a gloomy indication of the state of mind of Peking. Nehru has already reacted very strongly to it. The first is much more dangerous, and might at any moment involve the UN forces in armed conflict with formed Chinese units, or force the UN air forces to bomb airfields in Manchuria. The repercussions of that are really alarming. I still find it hard to believe that the Chinese really wish to extend the conflict, and the U.S. gov[ernmen]t certainly doesn't want to. There seems however to be a real risk that the Chinese will seriously miscalculate the consequences of intervention, & that US opinion will make it very hard for the administration not to react in some way which will take us to the edge of a major flare up in the east. So far as I can see, this might suit the USSR quite well, by embroiling China with the west, and keeping major US forces engaged in a theatre which is of very little interest to them.

So far all is speculation. We here in New York are not likely to have much say in what is done. London is sure to urge the greatest caution, and I think the State Dep[artmen]t (though not necessarily the Pentagon) will probably be in full agreement. Whatever happens is bound to affect our proceedings here, since a number of Far Eastern items, such as Formosa[,] are shortly due to come up, & a delegation from Peking is to be present at the debates ...

Younger's anxieties were to be confirmed in the weeks that followed. In the next entry of his diary, dated 19 November 1950, he wrote:

What I wrote about the Assembly entering a new phase[44] is, I think[,] going to prove true, but the transition is occurring slowly. The Republicans gained in the [American mid-term] elections,[45] with the result, at least for the time being, that Acheson is again under fire, and there is pressure for a 'tougher' policy in the Far East. In the meantime Chinese communist intervention in Korea is well established, but only on a so-called 'volunteer' basis. No one yet knows how far they intend to go. It still looks to me as if on the one hand they are almost unalterably hostile to the US, & no longer believe they have much chance of getting into [the] UN in the near future; but on the other hand they do not want to commit themselves so deeply in Korea as to involve themselves in large scale hostilities, with mass bombing of Chinese cities. However, one's opinion is scarcely more than guesswork. The Chinese delegation is now on its way to N[ew] Y[ork], but has got no farther than Prague & doesn't seem to be hurrying. Pending their arrival, the Security Council debate is hanging fire, & our items on the Chinese situation, including Formosa, are temporarily adjourned, in the hope that once the Chinese are here it may be possible to make sense of the whole thing. At present the greatest danger is that something will happen in Korea, e.g. large scale air intervention from Manchuria against UN troops, which will precipitate retaliation against forces or places on Chinese soil.

The situation is very tense, and one feels pretty helpless at the moment, owing to the lack of contact with the Chinese. We are trying to make contact in Peking, but our man there[46] usually has difficulty in getting access to Chou En-lai[47] and in discussing high policy matters at all. Whether we will do any better in New York when the [Chinese] delegation arrives is still quite uncertain. In the meantime one cannot even make intelligent guesses at what is going to happen . . .

Younger continued to be preoccupied by the problem of communist China when he wrote the next entry in his diary on 26 November 1950.

. . . The last week at [the] UN has been partly marking time awaiting the Chinese communists who have now arrived. Next week may therefore see some clarification of their intentions. In the meantime, they appear to have halted their advance into Tibet, & have certainly not reinforced N[orth] Korea any more. A 'final' offensive has just begun there[48] which, it is hoped, will clear the whole country up to the frontier in a few days. If it does, the situation in N[ew] Y[ork] should be favourable for negotiations. On the other hand, if there is bitter resistance & slow progress or – even worse – further reinforcements from Manchuria, things will look black.

At the moment the main trouble is a widening of the gap between US & UK policy. U.S. opinion has been 'hardening' & we are being accused of 'appeasement'. I do not think there is justification for this. The word 'appeasement' is coming to be used for any attempt to reach agreement. The basic trouble, which has lain at the back of all our Far Eastern divergences, is the dogmatic belief of nearly all Americans that it is mere wishful thinking to hope for *any* accommodation with communists – whether Russian or Chinese. Basically they expect to have to fight them, & there is a big school of thought which thinks 'the sooner the better.' In consequence they have now virtually decided to prevent Formosa from getting into communist hands indefinitely. This may cause a good deal of difficulty, because it is likely that any real détente between [the] US & communist China will be dependent on the Chinese getting *some* satisfaction over Formosa. I don't see the Americans giving it to them. Nor do I yet know what London's policy is going to be. I am not much impressed either with the consistency of London's thinking at the moment, or with their arrangements for cooperation with Washington. There seems to be considerable lack of coordination at the present time . . .

As Younger was writing this entry, the Chinese forces in Korea launched a massive and overwhelming counter-attack in the area of the Changjin reservoir at the centre of the UN front which caught their opponents by surprise. By 28 November 1950, the US and UN commander in Korea, General Douglas MacArthur, cabled his superiors in Washington that

> [a]ll hope of localisation of the Korean conflict to enemy forces composed of North Korean troops with alien token elements can now be completely abandoned. The Chinese military forces are committed in North Korea in great and ever increasing strength. No pretext of minor support under the guise of volunteerism or other subterfuge now has the slightest validity. We face an entirely new war.[49]

In his next diary entry, on 4 December 1950, Younger recorded his reaction to the unfolding disaster.

This has been a disastrous week. The worst of the alternatives which I forecast in my last entry has come to pass, but in a graver form than even I had feared. It seems that MacArthur's intelligence had entirely failed him, or else (as is possible) he refused to face facts which were put before him. Anyway after a day or so of his offensive, he suddenly announced that he had met, head on, a counter-offensive of 270,000 Chinese Communist troops. Since then figures of all sizes have been bandied around, & the only solid incontrovertible fact is that the U.N. forces have been overwhelmed & are everywhere in retreat. Already tonight the news is that *no line* can be held anywhere in Korea, only a couple of bridgeheads, if that.

This evening, Gladwyn[50] & I & Ernie Gross[51] & Jack Ross[52] spent a gloomy hour arguing whether the item on Chinese intervention in Korea should be immediately transferred to the Assembly from the Security Council where it had been vetoed.[53] They feel strongly that some joint US–UK initiative is vital within [the] UN, both in order to show the world that [the] UN is still in the picture and in order to stem the rising tide of propaganda which is seeking to divide [the] US & [the] UK.

We have agreed to do this, but on the understanding that we do not want the item discussed until Truman & Attlee have met in Washington & talked. They are due to do this tomorrow & it will no doubt take a couple of days before any clear decision can be taken.

At a press conference on 30 November 1950, President Truman had given the impression not only that the use of atomic weapons in Korea was under consideration, but that the decision to use them might be delegated to General MacArthur. This caused consternation in London, where the House of Commons was in the middle of a debate on foreign affairs, and the Prime Minister, who was under great pressure from his party, immediately requested and obtained Truman's agreement to an urgent meeting in

Washington. Since Bevin's health would not permit him to fly, Attlee made the trip without his Foreign Secretary.

Younger's diary entry of 4 December 1950 continues:

From our point of view the danger is that in the Assembly a charge of [Chinese] 'aggression' will be made, &, if made, inevitably voted. It will then follow that we are, in effect, at war with China & ought to take whatever sanctions are possible.

There is, of course, nothing more we can do militarily in Korea,[54] but such a situation would make any peaceful settlement with the Chinese impossible, would raise the whole question of Hong Kong, & would involve at least the risk of spreading the war & perhaps bringing Russia in. These things may be forced upon us by Russo-Chinese action, but we certainly ought to do nothing which would bring on such a catastrophe.

Concurrently with all this the Chinese communists in N[ew] Y[ork], headed by Gen[eral] Wu,[55] are beginning slowly to show signs of willingness to get in contact. One cannot yet say that they are ready to settle Korea on any acceptable terms; their intentions are as yet quite unknown; but they *may* be ready to compromise. If they are, in the present military situation it will be very tempting for many countries to do a deal. The real difficulty may well be that the only deal which shows any prospect of meeting Chinese wishes is for [the] U.S. to let the Communists have Formosa. That issue will be a good one on which to split [the] US from Europe & from [the] UK, for none of us have as yet subscribed to the US attitude on Formosa.

If a basic difference of view should develop between [the] US & ourselves, Formosa is, I think, likely to be part of the *immediate* cause. The *underlying* cause will probably be that we & the Europeans know that in an early world war Europe (and possibly Britain) will be indefensible, while the Americans, though they of course know this too, are much less affected by it. To them it is a relatively remote conception by comparison with the immediate humiliation in the Far East; to British & Europeans it is life & death.

All this is very crudely put, & is very incomplete as an analysis. I put it down as a summary of my thought in the midst of events. The future may just as well prove it wrong as right.

At the moment one does not feel much inclined to get into the question of blame. I still think it was right to send UN troops to Korea; also probably right to cross [the] 38th parallel. I doubt if we should ever have gone *much* beyond [the] 38th parallel; I never knew when or why the decision to go pretty well up to the border was taken.[56] As regards the final offensive, one does not know how far it was responsible for setting off the Chinese counter-move. That might have occurred anyway. When I heard that it was going to happen,[57] my immediate reaction was that it was OK if, & only if, it was sure to succeed rapidly. In the light of events it seems hard to resist the conclusion that, so far from this being sure, it was a pure gamble, taken without regard for consequences. Everyone knew the Chinese had vast manpower nearby to use if they chose. Presumably MacA[rthur] entirely misjudged his capacity to resist if the manpower *was* thrown in. It seems a colossal military blunder which justifies all the fears that have been expressed about MacA[rthur] as a dangerous megalomaniac.

A further interesting little sidelight on MacA[rthur] is that when one of our embassy people pressed Dean Rusk of the State Dep[artmen]t[58] to call for more operational reports from Korea, Rusk said the Department was reluctant to press the General for more reports than he wanted to give, since 'he would only invent them'!

The next entry in Younger's diary is dated 11 December 1950, and gives his impression of the Truman–Attlee talks, in which he briefly participated, as well as an account of the efforts in the United Nations to secure a ceasefire in Korea.

In the last week the Truman–Attlee talks have occurred, the Chinese offensive has slowed down in Korea, somewhere around the 38th parallel, and we are about to debate a cease-fire resolution, to be introduced by the Indians.

I was present at the second day of the Washington talks on Dec[ember] 5th.[59] The P.M. was very good, as he always is on Asian questions. Franks[60] was good too. Between them they seemed to be making some small impression on the Americans, but not enough to make any real difference to US policy in the short run. If we can buy time, there may be some effect.

The President let Acheson do all the talking, & only made a few comments, mostly quite good. Acheson was, I thought, a bit rigid & blinkered in his thinking. Our differences go pretty deep & are due to quite different appreciations of the nature of Chinese communism and nationalism, and of the possibility of 'eliminating communism' which appears to be the American intention. I find their whole conception, military and political, half-baked & disastrous.

The difference crystallises in the question whether, as the price of peace in the Far East, we are prepared to recognise the position of the new China in the world. We can do this by ceasing to support Chiang Kai Shek in Formosa, and by letting the communists take their place in [the] U.N. If neither of these things is done (& the Americans still find both unacceptable) I do not see how the communists can be expected to believe that the Korean operation is anything but a part of a US plan for preventing the fulfilment of the Chinese revolution. If that is the true US intention (and I myself believe that at the moment it is), then I see no peaceful way out of the Korean affair. If we can get a temporary cease-fire, & it then becomes clear to the world that there is a peaceful way open to us if, & only if, we are prepared to give China some satisfaction, then it is possible that [the] US might be forced to take a more reasonable & practical view. That is, I think, the importance of our maintaining pressure upon all our US contacts, so as to 'soften them up' in preparation for a climb-down which they may have to make. This analysis does not offer a very bright hope, but I see no other. I expect the Chinese to be exceedingly difficult so long as their military situation is strong. The Russians are sure to stiffen them up as much as possible.

It was in this situation that 13 Asian states made an appeal to the Chinese & N[orth] Koreans not to go beyond the 38th parallel[61] & later introduced a cease-fire resolution – or rather a tentative proposal for the President [of the General Assembly] & 2 others to explore the military conditions for a cease-fire. The Americans have been exercising great pressure to ensure that the door should not be opened, even *after* the cease-fire, to discussion of Formosa or the representation of Peking. We nearly got into a major row with them, because we told the Asian group, through Rau,[62] that we were in favour of an immediate call for [a] cease-fire, and were prepared to consider wider negotiations later. In the end the row never materialised, but only because the Asian group gave way to US pressure & never put forward the sort of resolution to which the Americans objected.

There is not now a very high hope that the Chinese will accept a cease-fire except in conjunction with a wider settlement. The only real hope is that fighting may actually stop, & that no one will want to restart it. After some delay there might then be a chance for negotiations of some kind gradually to start.

On his way back from Washington, Clem Attlee called for an hour or so at [the] U.N. and then had a commonwealth dinner party at Gladwyn [Jebb]'s house before going on to Canada.[63] His visit was a great success & he seemed both well & fairly satisfied with his visit.

In the meantime the situation of [the] U.N. forces in Korea is a bit better. They are regrouping & have not had exceptional losses. British losses are slight. There may therefore be a chance for a settlement. My worst fear on that score is that every bit of good news makes the Americans less ready to reach agreement. It is certainly true that there is a strong war psychosis noticeable here. Rather than face unpleasant facts they are, basically, quite ready to face a widening war. It is a dangerous mood, & a large section of the press is fostering it. Many people have the impression that the ordinary American is a good deal less bellicose than either the politicians or the press, & is even beginning to think that the British may have been right & may still be able to do something to prevent war. Official opinion, however, as represented by Ernie Gross & Jack Ross who are our main contacts, is so sceptical of any possible agreement that it gives little thought of trying to increase the chances of agreement, and concentrates instead on ensuring that 'the record' shall look satisfactory after all hope of agreement has been given up. One notices all sorts of little signs of this in the tactical discussions we have with them about the order & tempo of events. I doubt if they are fully conscious of their own motives. They are very earnest well intentioned men & I am sure they think they are doing everything they can to make agreement possible, but in fact they are constantly trying to rush things & to promote debate at unsuitable moments when there is nothing to be gained and every chance of foolish things being said in public which will increase the tension.

Younger was not alone in believing that 'a strong war psychosis' existed in the United States. Field-Marshal Sir William Slim, who was the Chief of the Imperial General Staff and who had accompanied Attlee to Washington, told his colleagues on the British Chiefs-of-Staff committee on 14 December 1950 that

> [t]he United States were convinced that war was inevitable, and that it was almost certain to take place within the next eighteen months; whereas we did not hold this view, and were still hopeful that war could be avoided. This attitude of the United States was dangerous because there was the possibility that they might think that since war was inevitable, the sooner we got it over the better, and we might as a result be dragged unnecessarily into world war III.[64]

The 1950 session of the General Assembly was coming to an end and Younger was at last able to return home. He wrote the next entry in his diary, dated 17 December 1950, on the plane back to London.

... The Assembly adjourned two days ago having passed the resolution setting up a little 'cease-fire group' under Entezam[,] the other members being Rau and Pearson[,][65] to discuss practical steps with the Chinese & the [U.N.] unified command. There is at present no reason to think that the Chinese will agree to a cease-fire on any other terms than withdrawal of UN troops (which they insist on describing as US troops) from Korea, and a settlement of Formosa & admission of their gov[ernmen]t to [the] U.N. *Our* line, which is also hinted at in the resolution, is that these other questions can be discussed as soon as fighting stops in Korea, but that none of us can accept the Chinese proposition that the whole Korean operation is merely a US aggression, etc. etc.

I saw Wu & his 'éminence grise', Chiou,[66] for half-an-hour on Friday[67] & he said categorically that he will not even speak to the ceasefire group. He intends to leave for Peking on Tuesday.[68] I am afraid the prospects of any settlement are at present poor. It is just possible that they may revive if the military situation goes on improving in Korea and the Chinese begin to think that it may after all be difficult to drive us completely out of the country. That is one reason why we are trying to play for time & keep the cease-fire group alive long enough to give a chance of a change in Korea. That is one reason why I am going home. It is a way of showing Ernie Gross that I don't envisage *any* early proposals being put through the Assembly which would bring us to a state of war with China. Nearly everyone in [the] UN, except the Americans and a few irresponsible Latin Americans[,] share our caution and are in no hurry for heroic decisions. One strong point in our argument which I make constantly to Ernie [Gross] (and never feel that he has appreciated) is that in the meantime nothing which could be done in a military sense is being held up for want of authority from [the] U.N. There is therefore nothing 'weak' in wishing to delay fateful decisions pending thorough consideration of consequences. I am afraid that thinking about consequences beyond the immediate step is, at present, a thoroughly 'un-American activity.'[69] Indeed the process that is going on here in the press & in political circles, & even I think in the State Department, is one of feeling rather than thinking. The atmosphere moreover is not improved by the fact that Acheson is again heavily under fire & is likely to be forced out, perhaps in favour of Dulles.

I should derive little comfort from the appointment of Dulles. As a man I infinitely prefer Acheson. It may be, however, that a more or less moderate Republican like Dulles would be better able to resist the extremists than Acheson, & might therefore even prove more capable of basing his policy upon the merits of the situation than Acheson. It is a lamentable position in any event.

I spent all the week engaged on the Korean question. I only made one or two minor interventions in committee. This is not a moment for making big speeches. We are all waiting upon events, & for the moment the less said the better.

Younger did his best to try to influence American opinion. His diary entry continues with accounts of dinners with important representatives of the US print and broadcast media and of the Congress of Industrial Organisations, one of the two main American trade union federations,[70] at which he sought to explain the situation as he saw it. The entry concludes with some reflections on his own performance, and that of the rest of the British delegation to the United Nations, over the previous three months.

... So that's the end of the General Assembly (though it may reconvene in Jan[uary]). I began it frankly a bit scared & rather dreading it. I end it pretty well satisfied. Discounting all the flattery & ballyhoo I know I have done fairly well. I think the delegation found me adequate as a leader & chairman, & after an uncertain start the thing ran well. My speeches were nearly all quite well received, without being in any way sensational. (I do not think sensational debating efforts would have been appropriate this year in any case). What is equally important is that in the lobbies & behind the scenes I felt that I 'went down' . So did my colleagues. Indeed I think that any lack of brilliance on our part was fully compensated by the very satisfactory way in which nearly all of us got on with other delegations. Both the politicians and the advisers deserve credit for this ...

The permanent delegation, whose main members are Gladwyn [Jebb], John Coulson and Dennis Laskey, is pretty good, & certainly very intelligent. Gladwyn has been over-lionised by the U.S. public, & may perhaps be becoming rather too much of a prima donna, but that, I think, will pass & is in any case not mainly his fault. John Coulson (and his wife Mavis) are *very* nice. He is above all a career diplomat & will probably never set the Thames on fire, but I have seldom felt more quiet confidence in anyone as an adviser. He is absolutely without personal vanities or touchiness or intellectual dishonesty, & gives one a feeling of rock like sanity which is very comforting.

Outside the Assembly my various appearances were, I think, rather specially successful. Anyway they seemed so to me . . .

In general I feel that these three months have enlarged my experience and increased my stature quite a bit. I certainly feel rather more confidence in myself, and more able to take responsibility than I did before. Whether I shall still find this when I get home is another matter. I think [the] UN & [the] USA are an easy context in which to shine. The House [of Commons], or even one's constituency (let alone one's friends) are a far stiffer test.

The last entry in Younger's diary for the year is appropriately dated 31 December 1950.

. . . Little political news. No progress in N[ew] Y[ork] over Korea. I saw Ernie B[evin] a couple of times & thought him unwell, discouraged & without ideas. Very depressing.

I wanted to see Nye [Bevan], but he has been in Wales.

So far as I can gather people here seem fairly satisfied with the way things were handled at Lake Success.[71] Politically, I think I can say I have had a pretty good year. I have certainly had a lot of experience in a short time.

3 From Bevin to Morrison, January–March 1951

The new year brought no signs of improvement in the international situation. In particular, events in Korea continued to give rise to anxiety and precipitated a major crisis in Anglo-American relations. In his next diary entry, dated 7 January 1951, Younger wrote:

> ... The international situation is peculiarly worrying and depressing at the moment. As I write, we have reached the point where the UN 'Cease-fire group'[1] have reported failure (though it is said that Rau is making a fresh proposal) & the Chinese have launched their expected second offensive[2] below the 38th parallel. They are being pretty successful, so much so that we all doubt whether the U.S. military really intend to hold on in Korea at all. (Jimmy[3] is out there with the 27th [Commonwealth] B[riga]de) & writes home in most scornful terms of the US troops around him).
>
> Whether we hold in Korea or not, the Americans want a [UN] resolution condemning China as an aggressor, to be followed by whatever sanctions are practicable, notably blockade, withdrawal of diplomatic representation, and possibly the promotion of subversive activity based upon the Nationalists in Formosa.[4] H[is] M[ajesty's] G[overnment] think this a futile programme, which will do virtually no harm to China, but may well precipitate serious trouble for us, both in the Far East (Hong Kong) and possibly in Europe. Moreover it will almost certainly not get the support of Asian countries, notably India[,] & will thus split both [the] UN and the Commonwealth.
>
> In this situation one can feel nothing but depression when one contemplates the quality of the leadership which is likely to be given by [the] US and the Commonwealth.
>
> [The] United States is of course bound to give the main lead, by virtue of her power & her position in Japan & [the] F[ar] E[ast]. So far, with the exception of her decision to resist N[orth] Korean aggression in June (which I still think was right) she has hardly done or said a sensible thing over many months. By linking Formosa with Korea; by refusing to recognise Peking & by clinging to Chiang Kai Shek; by the rashness of M[a]cArthur's military policy in Korea; and finally by the failure of any of her troops except the [First] Marine Division to fight properly,[5] she could not have played

more completely into the hands of the Russians, or made it more certain that [the] USSR & China will be united in an expansionist policy in the Far East in the immediate future. Having been largely responsible for getting us into this dangerous situation, she is pressing for measures which may make it more dangerous still, without offering any prospect of putting effective pressure on [the] USSR or China. When you add to this, that simultaneously she has been pressing for immediate German rearmament, regardless of the risk of provoking the Russians at the moment of Europe's greatest weakness, you could scarcely get a more complete picture of dangerous stupidity on the part of a leading power. On the German issue we have now, I think, persuaded her to go slow, & the damage *may* not have been done. In the east, however, I fear that most of the milk is already spilt; the Chinese have been driven into full hostility, and – what is equally dangerous – a realisation of the strength of their position. If they now feel inclined to take Hong Kong & Indo-China I very much doubt whether we or [the] US can do anything about it at all.[6]

At the moment we are refusing to give up hope, and are trying to prevent the Americans from pursuing their policy of 'limited war' against China. I have been trying to persuade the gov[ernmen]t to speak very brutally about it, lobby against the Americans at Lake Success,[7] & also to try to get a combined front with the Commonwealth Prime Ministers who are at present in conference in London.[8]

It is on this that I am depressed about our own government. Although the whole Cabinet is solid on the merits of the policy, there is great reluctance to be tough with the Americans about it. So far we have done little more than express our view to the Americans. We have given them no cause to think that, if they disregard us, we will cause them any trouble. Nor have we made any public statement either officially, or by calculated press leakage, of our position. The consequence is that we have, in effect, brought no pressure on the Americans at all, & I doubt if we will do so. I do not yet know what the Commonwealth P.M.s are going to say, but I have little hope of their being prepared to bring any pressure either, despite the fact that they all think the American line wrong. Nehru of course has no inhibitions about speaking out, but his views have little effect on America.

I have already gone as far as I possibly can in pressing my view. I first put it to Ernie Bevin.[9] He obviously disliked it but did not rule it out. However, he took me along next day to see the P.M. & I got the chance to say it all over again to him. He made practically no comment, except that when Ernie wailed almost tearfully that this was the end of the US/UK alliance, the P.M. pulled him up rather sharply and said he did not think so at all. I tried to get the P.M. to say whether we were *in any event* prepared to vote for the limited sanctions that [the] US are proposing & to tell the Americans privately *now* that we were *not* prepared to do so, but I could not get him to go so far. In the end we did send a telegram to Washington telling Franks to tell Acheson that our support for a resolution condemning

China as an aggressor, & calling for consequent measures, could *not* be assumed.[10] That is the most I could get.

My impression of Ernie has been lamentable. Sometimes he seems very unwell, sometimes not so bad; but every time I have seen him so far he has seemed to me to be morally a broken man. I think the weakness is partly physical, & that he simply hasn't the stamina for taking difficult decisions. Just now the line of least resistance is to drift along behind the Americans, making ineffectual protests all the way. That is certainly what Ernie would do. What the P.M. & the Cabinet will do is likely to depend, I suppose, very largely on the Commonwealth view. Since the Commonwealth will probably be split, I suspect that in the end we will just go along with the Americans. In the absence of Cripps[11] I know no one who is likely to show much courage but Nye [Bevan]. I believe Hector [McNeil] shares my view, but I wouldn't expect any of the leading ministers to have a line of their own. Others not in the Cabinet, such as John Strachey[12] & George Strauss[,][13] would be another story.

Actually I do not myself know yet just how far *I* am prepared to go ... What I don't know is whether, in the event of the Americans going ahead in spite of us, I am prepared to refuse support in public, & in particular refuse to take part in sanctions against China. This would be a major breach with the Americans, and it would probably do little or nothing to protect Hong Kong or Indo-China from attack, now that the Americans have brought matters to such a pitch. Moreover it is argued that a breach of this kind would play into the hands of the isolationists & might easily lead to [the] U.S. not sending more troops to Europe.

All this is possible, though I think exaggerated. Against it, is the prospect that the Asian states would refuse to cooperate (I cannot see India or Burma or Indonesia applying a blockade to China). India would probably maintain her Ambassador in Peking and so would dissociate herself from U.N. policy (assuming there had been the requisite majority).

Many people think that it would also lead the Communist states leaving [the] UN, which would then become in effect an anti-communist alliance pure & simple. That in turn would lead to the defection of a number of Asian (& perhaps other) states & [the] UN would be at an end.

An equally big question is whether action of this kind against China would be considered by Russia to make eventual world war so certain that she would decide to move in Europe soon. Everyone agrees that there would at present be no counter to a Soviet move in force in Europe. Presumably the Americans would want to atom-bomb Russia (no doubt from UK bases), but whatever that might do to Russia, it would not prevent the Red Army from reaching the Channel ports. Once that had happened, the Americans would have to consider whether to drop atom bombs on W[estern] Europe too! I suspect they *would* bomb the Ruhr, but not France – anyway at first.

How big is the risk of setting all this in motion through rash action in the east, is very hard to say. If [the] USA succeeded in leading the Western nations and the Commonwealth into war with China, I think a Russian might well take that as a certain pointer to world war within a few years. On that assumption, she [Russia] might prefer to deny W[estern] Europe to the Americans *now*, while it can be easily done, rather than wait until the Atlantic pact has begun to mean something in real military strength.

I think it quite likely that Russia would react in this way if the Americans allowed a large part of their forces to get tied up in the east. The opportunity might then seem altogether too good to miss. If however the war with China was little more than a formal state of war & a naval block-ade, I do not feel certain that it would have much effect upon Soviet policy elsewhere. The most one can say is that it *might*, & as war with China is such a pointless affair anyway, it seems silly to take any risk on account of it.

Apart from the dangers of a 'limited war' with China, which were serious enough, Younger raised two other important issues: whether the Soviet Union might also become involved if the Korean War expanded; and, if so, what would be the role of the United States Air Force's bombers stationed on British soil?

As it happens, we do possess some information on what the Soviet Union's intentions were at this time. A conference of Soviet and East European communist leaders and defence ministers was held in Moscow from 9 to 12 January 1951. According to the contemporary account of the Romanian defence minister, Emil Bodnaras, Stalin opened the conference on the evening of 9 January by declaring:

The opinion arose in recent times that the United States is an invincible power and is prepared to initiate a third world war. As it turns out, however, not only is the US unprepared to initiate a third world war, but is unable even to cope with a small war such as the one in Korea. It is obvious that the US needs several more years for preparation. The US is bogged down in Asia and will remain pinned down there for several years. The fact that the US will be tied down in Asia for the next two or three years constitutes a very favorable circumstance for us, for the world revolutionary movement. These two-to-three years we must use skillfully ... Our task consists of using the two-to-three years at our disposal in order to create a modern and powerful military force ... You in the People's Democracies must, within two to three years, create modern and powerful armies that must be combat-ready by the end of the three-year period.

At the conclusion of the conference on 12 January 1951, Stalin made it clear that these military preparations were defensive. They were necessary, he said, because of the imperialists' way of thinking: they are in the habit of attacking unarmed or weakly armed countries in order to liquidate them, but they keep away from well-armed countries. This is why you need to arm during this respite, and arm well, in order that the imperialists respect you and keep away from you.[14]

There is another account of the same conference, which derives from Bodnaras' Czech counterpart, but while it confirms Stalin's insistence upon a three-year rearmament programme, it states that his intentions were aggressive.[15] In any event, Younger's fear that the Russians might take immediate advantage of the American involvement in Korea to seize Western Europe seems unfounded. Where he was surely right, however, was in believing that developments in Korea were rendering the international situation increasingly unstable.

In the event of a war with the Soviet Union, it was expected that American bombers based in Britain in would be used to attack Soviet targets. US Air Force B-29s had first been sent to Britain in 1948 at the time of the Berlin blockade, but these aircraft had not been modified to carry atomic bombs. A decision was taken in April 1950 to increase the number of American air bases in Britain from three to seven and, by the middle of the year, all B-29s deploying to Britain had been so modified. On 11 June 1950, which was before the outbreak of the Korean War, President Truman had also authorised the transfer to US air bases in Britain of eighty-nine sets of the non-nuclear components of atomic bombs, and the first were in place by the end of July. More importantly, at the time Younger was writing, there was no sharing of information between the Americans and the British concerning the targeting of nuclear weapons and no clear and firm agreement that the British government would be consulted before the bombs were armed and used, a situation which the Chief of the Air Staff, Marshal of the RAF Sir John Slessor, described as 'quite intolerable'. Neither problem was resolved during what remained of the Labour government's period in office. An agreement of sorts on consultation was reached between President Truman and Attlee's Conservative successor, Winston Churchill, in January 1952, but full American agreement to joint targeting was not achieved until March 1957, although informal exchanges of information had begun in 1952.[16]

Younger's diary entry for 7 January 1951 continues:

The state of feeling about all this in this country is hard to gauge. Apart from educated people who are interested in foreign policy, I doubt if anyone has been much interested until the last few weeks. Now they are a bit scared, and their first reaction is one of resentment at the way [the] U.S. has ignored our advice & let us in for a war we don't want. Generally, people are still sticking their heads in the sand & are not facing the future realistically. In the labour movement, according to all I hear, morale would not be too good if further efforts were called for on account of trouble with China. No one really feels it is our war. Most people, if not everyone, feel that to call the Chinese 'aggressors', *tout court*, is a big over-simplification. They feel that this war is not required to support the principles of [the] UN, & is simply a US–Chinese quarrel. This is, I think, quite correct to the extent that this war would not be going on at all but for US policy *outside* [the] UN, especially with regard to Formosa.

Public and party opinion was indeed becoming more anxious. A Gallup poll taken in January 1951 showed that 58 per cent of those questioned felt that there was 'much danger' of a war compared with only 14 per cent the previous October. From 16 January to 12 February 1951, moreover, large numbers of foreign policy resolutions from constituency parties and other organisations poured into Labour Party headquarters, all of which urged the government to oppose American policy in the Far East. Newspapers such as *The Times*, the *Observer* and the *Manchester Guardian* were also critical of the United States.[17]

Concluding his long and somewhat repetitive diary entry of 7 January 1951, Younger reverted to his concern about the Foreign Secretary, Ernest Bevin.

... My worst anxiety at present is my lack of confidence in Ernie. I believe he would like simply to follow Acheson quietly, because he has as good as said so in an office meeting. He also said that if we didn't go with the Americans on this 'we would be letting the Americans down.' That is of course what republican columnists have been saying in the States, & when any of them have said it to me I have bitten them! I was pretty rude to Ernie, & only restrained myself because there were half-a-dozen officials present.

So far the office has been pretty good on this, but I can see that the 'don't be rude to the Americans' school is gaining. I don't think anyone, except perhaps Rob Scott,[18] is likely to stick to his guns very firmly.

I have noted this at some length, because I am at the moment uneasily poised between conflicting states of mind & can therefore write with some objectivity. I may soon have to burn my boats. Alternatively, as so often happens, events may turn out so that the straight issue never arises at all.

This was indeed what occurred, but not before a great deal more controversy and soul-searching on the part of Younger and his ministerial colleagues. Certainly nothing had been resolved by the date of his next diary entry, which was 21 January 1951.

A lot has happened in the last fortnight, & yet we are almost in the same place as regards the decision about China.

The Commonwealth P.M.s conference did far better than I had dared hope. It made a good public declaration[19] about the world situation in general, and also privately induced the U.S. to support a further approach to the Chinese by the cease-fire group. The approach was duly made and the Chinese made an ungracious & unforthcoming reply a few days ago.[20] Opinions differ as to whether it should be taken as a flat rejection or as a step in negotiations. We & the Canadians are both trying to obtain further clarification in Peking.

The Americans, on the other hand, did not even wait for an hour before announcing that the reply was a flat refusal & that [the] UN must denounce the Chinese as aggressors & consider further action. After much consultation we could not agree a resolution which we & the Commonwealth could all sponsor. The Americans were under too much pressure to wait, and have now put in a resolution which is milder than they originally intended, but nevertheless names the Chinese as aggressors and establishes the principle that sanctions (not of course confined to Korea) are called for, even if in practice it is found that nothing useful can be done at the moment.[21]

This resolution we have so far refused to co-sponsor. So have the Canadians & French. The Asian states are mostly opposed to it altogether. Tomorrow the cabinet has to decide finally (a) whether to sponsor after all (b) whether to vote for it, without sponsoring, or to abstain, and (c) in any case what line to tell Gladwyn [Jebb] to take when he speaks.

I really do not know what the decision will be. Many people will say that to desert the Americans now will be a major break and will prejudice our cooperation everywhere. I cannot honestly say that I think this will not happen. It might. And if it did happen it might be disastrous, on the assumption that without US aid Europe is likely to be overrun by the Red Army.

Nevertheless, on balance I am at present in favour of taking these risks. I do not really believe that the action proposed would upset the Anglo-American alliance for more than a short time. After a spasm of rage, I think the Americans would revert to the policy which their national interest dictates. I am also inclined to think that if we do stand firm now, the effect upon the Russians will probably be to make them less rather than more inclined to attack western Europe. I have always doubted whether that is part of their plan. If it had been they could have done it already & I think they will probably undertake it only if they think that the Americans + a rearmed Germany are busy building up forces which will eventually threaten the Soviet Union. In other words the Soviet attitude, however offensive, is basically defensive in origin.

It is very hard indeed to feel any confidence in these conclusions. There is little evidence which points decisively either way, and no matter which decision one takes, there is a very great risk involved. Certainly the bull-headed American policy both in Europe and in the east involves very high risks of early war, and little counterbalancing defensive force within say two years – by which time their clumsiness may well have brought things to a head. I very much doubt whether the populations of Europe or Britain would respond with the necessary determination if they were called upon for great sacrifices to meet such a situation. At the moment there is certainly no enthusiasm, while there is great distrust & resentment of United States policy, and especially of the neglect of the Americans to pay any attention to our views. This is not a good mood in which to approach a major effort of rearmament & military service.[22]

One further reason why I think this may be the moment at which to assert our independence of [the] USA in foreign policy is that the Americans have clearly reached the frame of mind in which they count upon us always to 'go along' with them, no matter what our misgivings. We have got to stop this rot if we ever want to have real influence upon them, and we are not likely to get a better chance than this of doing so. We know that on the merits the whole Commonwealth and the whole of western Europe is with us. The only question is whether they will have the nerve to stand up publicly for their views. Even if some of them go with the Americans, therefore, they will secretly admire our stand & will not be at all inclined to disregard us in future. Rather the reverse.

As we may have a number of even more crucial contests just ahead of us, e.g. on German rearmament, it is important not to acquire the habit of last-minute surrender. If we do the Americans will pay no attention to us – and rightly.

This is a very hard decision & I don't know which way it will go. Nye [Bevan],[23] to whom I spoke today[,] agrees with me, only more so. Ernie B[evin] and the office were both sound yesterday, but I don't trust their stamina, least of all Ernie's. I would expect the P.M. to be basically in agreement with us, but I would feel no confidence in the Cabinet as a whole. I am afraid that 'America right or wrong' is a very powerful sentiment among them.

The Cabinet meeting on 22 January 1951 did not in fact take a decision on the US resolution on China. Bevin told his colleagues that recent information from Washington indicated that the United States was not intending to ask for military action against the Chinese mainland, but wished to explore the possibility of economic sanctions. His advice, which was accepted by the Cabinet, was to defer any decision until the British representative in Beijing had reported the results of his further enquiries concerning the Chinese attitude towards a possible ceasefire.[24]

On the same day, however, Bevin fell ill with pneumonia and Younger once more found himself in charge at the Foreign Office. This gave him a unique opportunity to press for the adoption of his own more assertive policy towards the Americans. His next diary entry, dated 28 January 1951, records what happened.

... My main preoccupation has been and still is the vote on the U.S. Korean resolution at Lake Success. Just after my last entry the Chinese gave us & the Canadians an explanation which went a long way to show willingness to negotiate. At the same time military events in Korea, where the Chinese advance has petered out & actually gone into reverse, are favourable to negotiation.[25]

The Americans however at once declared the whole thing a fraud & a sham & have been trying to force their resolution through. Everyone is of course very reluctant to agree to condemnation, sanctions etc. when the door is still so obviously open for a further attempt at [a] peaceful settlement. All the Commonwealth & W[estern] Europe are with us on the merits, but all of them as I expected are going to go with the Americans in the last resort.

After every kind of effort to obtain changes in the US resolution, the Cabinet on Thursday[26] had to face the decision how to tell Gladwyn to vote on the unamended resolution. In the meantime the P.M. had made a statement in the House [of Commons] on Tuesday[27] saying bluntly that we think there sh[oul]d be further negotiations, and that sanctions are premature. From my point of view the object of this was to commit H[is] M[ajesty's] G[overnment] publicly to negotiation. As a result the Cabinet on Thursday felt that we could not possibly support further actions which rule negotiation out & that we must at least abstain. In Cabinet that view got a large majority. On a decision whether to abstain or to vote against, to my surprise the latter won. I spoke in favour of it & was, I think, quite effective. What I said was against the balance of F.O. opinion, and against what everyone thought Ernie would have done. I made both those points fully to the Cabinet.[28]

The division of opinion was interesting & typical. Jowitt,[29] Hector McNeil & Hugh Gaitskell were the only ones strongly in favour of supporting [the] US *at all costs*. The P.M. & Herbert [Morrison] wanted to abstain. Dalton, Addison,[30] Chuter [Ede], Jim Griffiths,[31] George Tomlinson,[32] Harold Wilson, Nye & even Tom Williams[33] all agreed to vote against! I was surprised and pleased, though I always knew that the decision was uncertain & might change, & so it turned out. I myself, though still firm on the main issue[,] am now rather inclined to think that abstention is good enough. On the other hand it was obviously wise to *threaten* to vote against, since it has scared the Americans who are frantically trying to devise compromises in order to get our vote.

On Friday[34] the Cabinet agreed to support an Israeli compromise, which, though not satisfactory, postpones sanctions until after a further attempt to negotiate.[35] This however the US Cabinet flatly rejected. They have however put forward one final offer of their own. This proposes that a committee should consider sanctions immediately but should not report so long as negotiations are going on. This I think would be *just* acceptable, provided they were genuinely prepared to negotiate.[36] So far they have shown no sign whatever of doing so & I am convinced they dread the very prospect of meeting the Chinese communists round a table.

I therefore recommended, & the P.M. agreed,[37] that we should tell the Americans we will take their amendment but only if they will assure us that they will not oppose proposals which Mike Pearson has been putting forward for an early conference.[38] This would be an earnest of their good faith & would enable the PM to justify to the British public his support of a US resolution which they will certainly not much like. It should also deprive the Chinese of any valid excuse for standing out of negotiations.

That is where we now stand. After a couple of days of tension between me and the chief office officials – Strang, Makins & Dixon, we are now pretty amicable & the only difference between us is whether we should now accept the US resolution so amended, even if they won't give us the assurances we want. They say yes. I, so far, say no. I say it partly on the merits, i.e. because I think if we let ourselves get bullied by [the] US this time we will never win again; and partly because I think that we will be in great trouble with a large section of the public if we vote with the U.S. & *then* they refuse reasonable negotiations.

The only further event, which is typical, is a statement by MacArthur in Korea[39] that now the 'stake is not Korea it is a free Asia.' I think this will prove very damaging both with Asians & our own people & perhaps with our own Cabinet tomorrow.

What a menace the man is! He has not only proved militarily rash &, at one stage at least[,] thoroughly incompetent, but he has also been totally disloyal both to the U.N. and even to the policy of his own government. While they and we were resolved to hold a line in Korea & to try to negotiate, he was busily pulling out of the whole country with a view to fighting a general war against China. This latest remark of his will arouse suspicion that even now he has not, as we had hoped, been fully disciplined.[40]

Although Younger's diary adds significantly to the official record of what transpired on 25 and 26 January 1951, it by no means tells the whole story. Another diarist, Hugh Gaitskell, informs us in detail of the backstairs negotiations which took place between the Cabinet meetings on those two dates and which led ministers to support the Israeli compromise.

As Younger recorded, Gaitskell had strongly advocated supporting the Americans in the Cabinet discussion on 25 January 1951. He was so angry at the decision to vote against the US resolution that he lobbied frantically with colleagues and officials to have the decision reversed. He even tried to convey a message to Bevin in hospital, but was informed that the latter was 'too incoherent to be told'. It was Strang who relayed news of the Israeli resolution to Gaitskell and suggested that this might prove 'a card of re-entry' with which to reopen the matter with Attlee. He then convinced Addison, who promised to talk to other ministers, before meeting up with Strang, Younger and Attlee at No. 10 Downing Street.

According to Gaitskell, 'they rapidly agreed that this [i.e. the Israeli resolution] was a new situation and the Cabinet would have to be called immediately'. He then urged Strang to set out what he thought Bevin would have done and to confirm that 'the Foreign Office people believed that there was a very big difference between abstention and voting against'. The diary entry makes clear that this was done deliberately in order to embarrass Younger, who was alleged to have told a different story at the key Cabinet meeting on 25 January 1951. There is, however, no warrant for this accusation. Not only did Younger assert the contrary in his own diary, but the Cabinet minutes of the meeting in question record him as stating that '[t]he Foreign Secretary had indicated at an earlier stage that in his opinion the United Kingdom ought in the last resort to vote for the United States resolution, but it had not been possible to take his view on the present situation.'[41]

Gaitskell then spoke with the Prime Minister alone. He does not say that Attlee agreed with him, but states that, after the new situation was explained to the Cabinet on 26 January 1951, the Prime Minister was 'quite firm' with the four remaining dissenters: Dalton, Bevan, Chuter Ede and Jim Griffiths.[42]

There is no trace of these machinations in the official records. This is, perhaps, not surprising and there is no reason to doubt the principal features of Gaitskell's intervention. What is less certain is the extent to which he was prepared to go to get his way. Prior to his meeting with the Prime Minister, Gaitskell had told one of his officials that he would threaten Attlee with his resignation if the decision to vote against the American resolution was not reversed. He confirmed that he had done so in a conversation with Dalton a month later.[43] A Prime Minister with a wafer-thin majority threatened with the resignation of his Chancellor of the Exchequer would indeed have faced a painful dilemma. There is, however, no hint of such a threat in Gaitskell's diary account of his conversation with Attlee.

The next entry in Younger's diary, which is dated 4 February 1951, begins with some concluding reflections on this problem in Anglo-American relations and goes on to discuss another: the question of German rearmament.

The issue of the US resolution was finally resolved, as dramatic issues so often are, by being blunted & whittled away by compromise. Although the Americans did not give quite the assurance for which we asked they gave an assurance of a sort that they would genuinely try to reach a peaceful settlement. On that the Cabinet agreed to vote for the amended US resolution.[44] We have now done so, & it was passed both in Committee and in the Assembly by 44–7. The Communist group, India & Burma voted against, & nearly all the other Asians abstained.[45]

I am worried about the decision. It is not a helpful resolution, & Peking has already said that it cannot now negotiate.[46] Nevertheless I agreed that we should support it, because it offers the only chance of getting the Americans and the Chinese round a table at all. I do not really think that the Chinese decision whether to negotiate or not will depend upon this vote. It will depend upon the military situation in Korea & upon China's long term plans and calculations in the Far East. If they have already decided not to negotiate, this resolution will of course give them a good excuse for break-ing. That is about the only effect it will have at that end. Here, however, it is causing grave misgivings in the Labour Party where our vote is pretty heavily criticised.[47]

As soon as that issue was past its crisis, another took its place – the attempt to get 4-power talks going and the government's policy on German rearmament. I had to present an F.O. paper to the Cabinet without having any chance of full discussion in the office. I disliked the paper, & so did the Cabinet, & I had a pretty rough morning.[48]

I will not write much about this at the moment. The whole subject is in an unholy muddle – largely, I think, through Ernie's fault. He has wavered from one view to another on German rearmament, first trying to delay it, then joining the Americans bullying the French for greater speed, then having cold feet about it & vainly thinking of going back. The whole thing has been inadequately explained to the Cabinet from time to time with the result that they are now shocked to find how far they have been committed. The Ameri-cans, on the other hand, who have been pushing ahead in their usual bull-headed manner, have not really been given any reason to think that we are still half-hearted & anxious for delay – which is clearly the actual position of the Cabinet at the moment. The French, having been subjected to great pres-sure not only by [the] US but by us too, now seem to have given up the fight and to be, if anything, more resigned than we are to a fairly rapid start to German rearmament. If therefore the Cabinet, worried by the undoubted reluctance of the Labour Party to accept the policy, now want to change the pace or alter the direction[,] I foresee great difficulty & pretty well justified annoyance on the American side, & even, perhaps, the French.

The attitude eventually taken on this will influence our approach to the 4 Power talks. In particular it will go far to determine what sort of a price we will insist on exacting from the Russians in return for a promise not to arm Germany. The American view, to which the office here seem to subscribe[,] is that we cannot give up German rearmament in return for anything less than a major détente, extending far beyond the German problem. If we are forced to stick on this, I think there will be great trouble in the party & even in the Cabinet. On the other hand, if we deadlock on this with the Ameri-cans, it will be a far graver matter than our threatened row over Korea.

My own views are not yet formed, and I have no time to write at length about them now. I expect to be giving a great part of my time to this subject in the immediate future.

Younger's views on German rearmament had, however, crystallised suffi-ciently to enable him to write a penetrating minute, dated 5 February 1951, on a Foreign Office paper which had just been submitted to the Chiefs-of-Staff. He saw a contradiction between the perceived need to rearm the Federal Republic of Germany and Britain's own defence preparations.

This paper argues, in the main convincingly, that although German rearmament is perhaps the biggest provocation we could offer to the Soviet Union, it is nevertheless unlikely that she will be induced thereby to forestall it by large-scale military operations, and in particular by the overrunning of Western Europe.

I am not concerned in this minute to quarrel with this argument in itself. What worries me about it is the difficulty of reconciling it with the assumptions we are making in relation to defence generally.

Paragraph 4. sets out the main reasons why the Soviet Union is unlikely to risk an early war. Practically all these reasons would equally support the thesis that the Soviet Union is unlikely to risk a large-scale war even in the remoter future. Although it is true that her air defence may improve and her atomic stockpile may grow, she surely cannot have much confidence that she will be able to prevent atomic destruction of the 'communist citadel' or that she can 'conquer the American continent' in say 1954 or 1957. If one is to assume, moreover, that by that time Western Germany will have been heavily rearmed, unimpeded by any major Soviet reaction, surely the temptation to the Russians to attempt the conquest of Western Europe will be less than today, not greater.

Yet our new defence programme has been based upon the assumption that it is necessary to arm to meet precisely this threat. Until a year ago, I understand, the dangerous date was put in 1957. The increased tension resulting from Korea brought the date forward to 1954. Since then, it has again come forward to 1952.[49]

When I asked why this last acceleration was thought necessary, I was told (a) that Korea had brought home to us what great risks the Russians are prepared to take to attain their ends, and (b) that the proposal for German rearmament, though necessary for the effective defence of the west, carried with it an increased risk that the Russians might launch an early preventive war.

I find (a) unconvincing. The Russians, I am sure, thought they were taking almost no risk in Korea in June. When the United States reaction showed that there were after all risks involved, the Russians were most cautious and have avoided involvement so carefully that we have not even caught them out in giving air assistance in Korea.[50]

I believe (b), coupled no doubt with the pressure of American hysteria, to be the real reason why the Chiefs of Staff have become more nervous of early war. This paper, however, suggests that it is not on balance a good reason. If therefore this paper is to be taken as a basis of policy, there seems little justification for the accelerated defence timetable.

On the other hand if this paper is wrong, and German rearmament must be considered likely to provoke an early war, it is hard to see what good German rearmament will do since ex hypothesi, the war is going to break out before German forces can possibly have made an effective contribution to Western defence.

There is one other point, relating to the scale rather than to the timing of the defence programme, which this paper raises in my mind.

The Korean experience showed the need for the West to increase its strength sufficiently to cope more effectively with limited adventures short of general war. Since these adventures might occur over a long period of so-called peace, it was necessary to limit the defence programme to a scale which would permit normal economic activity to go on in the United Kingdom. £3600 million in three years, less some United States aid, seemed just reasonable in this context.[51]

The new programme,[52] however, admittedly involves a quite different scale of effort and of dislocation of normal economic activity.[53] It will be hard to persuade the public that this effort can be maintained on the proposed scale over a long period of years. I doubt if they will think it necessary at all unless they are assured that there is a real possibility of major Soviet aggression at a fairly early date – say by 1954.

This paper, however, argues that even with maximum provocation (i.e. German rearmament) such aggression is improbable. One would have thought that a fortiori without the provocation, major aggression could be almost ruled out. Why then must the defence programme exceed the scale and tempo thought necessary last September?

This paper confirms me in the opinion, which I was already inclined to hold, that our thinking on German rearmament and defence is schizophrenic.[54]

Younger also presented a paper on German rearmament to the Cabinet on 7 February 1951,[55] although it is not clear how much of it was written by himself. It included a detailed history of the negotiations so far, from which the conclusion was drawn

> that the steps hitherto taken in regard to German rearmament ... do not constitute any final decision on the part of the Allied Governments (or, of course, on the part of the German Federal Government) either on the conditions for a German contribution or on the moment at which any agreed plan for raising German forces should be begun.

There was, however, 'a moral commitment' and 'all the steps taken up to the present moment have had the full concurrence of the Cabinet'.

The paper went on to point out that there was plenty of scope for delay. The negotiations with the Germans for a new agreement to replace the occupation statute, which were proceeding in parallel with those on rearmament, were bound to take time. The same was true for the negotiations on the formation of an integrated European army, which the French had insisted upon as a quid pro quo for their consent to German rearmament. In addition the newly appointed American supreme commander in Europe, General Eisenhower, had recently given the impression that he was not in favour of undue haste with German rearmament until the existing Atlantic pact forces were more substantial,[56] while the Federal German government itself was insisting on the need to convince the German people that allied forces in Germany had been substantially reinforced.

This paper was discussed by the Cabinet on 8 February 1951 and even the official minutes provide ample evidence of the rift inside the Labour government.[57] Fortunately, Eisenhower's statement enabled ministers to take refuge in a policy of delay, as Younger makes clear in the next entry in his diary, which is dated 25 February 1951.

... On 12th Feb[ruary] there was a foreign affairs debate in the House [of Commons], followed by a two day defence debate later that week. It was a difficult business getting policy sufficiently clarified for public presentation in time, especially on German rearmament.

The PM opened the debate, and I closed.[58] In the end it went off fairly smoothly. We owed that as much as anything to Eisenhower, who ended a tour of Europe by making a speech in which he appeared almost uninterested in German forces & put all his emphasis upon the prior build up of the other western countries. As that coincides exactly with our view here, we were able to take the same line, which allayed the fears of all sides, – both those (mainly Labour) who hate all idea of a German army, and those (mainly Tory) who feared that we were going to try to wriggle out of our earlier commitment 'in principle' in the Atlantic Council!

I did not play an important part in thrashing all this out. My main worry was caused by an unfortunate speech of [Sir Ivone] Kirkpatrick our High Commissioner in Germany which was understood as indicating an intention to reduce [the] sentences of war criminals in view of the changed circumstances.[59] This coincided with the release by the Americans of Alfred Krupp[60] & some other ex-Nazi industrialists. The combination of these two raised a fine storm in the press and in the Labour Party who got the impression, not altogether unnaturally, that we were prepared to pardon any Nazi criminal, especially the soldiers, in order to get a new German army into being.

Actually the whole thing was little more than unfortunate timing and a failure to realise the need to explain very fully what was being done. Kirkpatrick's remarks only contained one unfortunate phrase;[61] & the American decisions were taken on legal & not political grounds. There had in fact been no change of policy at all. Nevertheless the public was not altogether wrong in sensing that many powerful influences are at work to get Germans back into uniform and are quite willing to let bygones be bygones in the interests of the anti-communist crusade. The Catholics are prominent in this respect, & Kirkpatrick is a Catholic. That gave rise to a lot of prejudice (which I share in part) & the cabinet were out for his blood.[62] I defended him as best I could, & nothing very serious resulted. But my efforts were not enough to appease the office whose 'trade union' instincts were fully aroused by this attack on their colleague. They got at old Ernie, (who was convalescing in his flat) & he weighed in with the P.M. in a tone of indignation, & got rather a raspberry for his pains. It was a distinctly embarrassing little incident & brought out, for the first time in my experience, the deep dislike of the Foreign Office for the present government. One could sense all around one their feeling that the Cabinet were just a lot of cads who put the blame on officials as soon as things go wrong. They hadn't really much cause for complaint in that respect. Kirkpatrick behaved in a very petty way & by the end of it even his own colleagues were getting fed up with him.

The diary entry of 25 February 1951 continues with his descriptions of further encounters with two key figures, one of whom (Aneurin Bevan) represented, for Younger, the future of the Labour Party; and the other (Ernest Bevin) the past. On 15 February 1951, Bevan made the winding up speech for the government in the defence debate. According to Younger,

... Nye ... had a considerable triumph, with a rather quiet speech which delighted his own side & won admiration even from the Tory press.[63]

I was very glad about this, for I have been seeing a good deal of him lately, and am very conscious of the gulf that now separates him from most of his leading colleagues. I think the PM has a split mind about him, part distrust and part admiration. Others, especially Herbert Morrison, Bevin, Shinwell & some younger ones like Hector [McNeil], loathe him wholeheartedly. It is therefore very important that he should retain his hold upon the party in the house [of Commons] & in the country. I have no doubt myself that he is the outstanding figure of the political movement now, & he ought to have increasing weight in determining policy. Now that he is Minister of Labour, he will be more powerful, but in the inner circles in the Cabinet he is kept at arm's length as far as possible. He only forces his way in by virtue of his known reputation outside.

We had a very pleasant evening with him & Jenny[64] & Pat Ll[ewellyn]-D[avies][65] to whom we gave dinner one evening. He was in very good form – frivolous & sociable at first & later talking serious politics. He is a fascinating mind. I think he probably has that element of untrustworthiness which is attributed to Welshmen, and I cannot feel sure that one would really like him as a very close friend. I would have to know him better before being certain of that. I do know, however, that he is the only member of the Cabinet who seems to me to have the qualities of leadership & political vision. I think that the hope of the Labour Party renewing its vigour & having a fresh phase of development ahead of it depend mainly upon him. All the other senior people are extinct volcanoes, or else were never volcanoes at all!

... Ernie Bevin is now recovering at Eastbourne & is expected back at work in a week. Actually he cannot possibly do a full day's work when he returns. He looks & sounds weak & will only be able to handle a very few subjects.

I have seen him once, a week ago, & I had a depressing conversation. His egotism gets more monstrous as time goes on. He is eaten up with the thought that others are getting the credit which should be his. The papers (both right and left) are full of criticism of him & are urging Attlee to have a new Foreign Secretary. Ernie is convinced that every word of this is inspired by one or other of his colleagues. There is hardly one of them about whom he has not said bitter things to me. On this occasion it was Hartley Shaw-cross, Nye (of course) & finally even 'No. 10'. He didn't mention the P.M. by name, but he is clearly sore that the country should find Attlee more satis-factory as a foreign secretary than Ernie. I think they do.

When I came away from Ernie on this occasion I felt positively contami-nated by his petty bitterness. Whatever he may have been when he was a fit man he is a pretty pathetic old wreck now, & in many ways contemptible. I cannot think that he has any worthwhile contribution to make now. I think he could only be effective as a maker of trouble in the cabinet & the party . . .

By the time of the next entry in Younger's diary, which is dated 28 March 1951, Bevin had left the Foreign Office and been replaced by Herbert Morrison.[66]

. . . It was a rather painful transition when it came. Old Ernie may perhaps have become reconciled to giving up the job, but he had clearly not become reconciled to handing it over to his arch-enemy Herbert. He tried first to get Jim Griffiths appointed, then Hector McNeil. (The other talked of candidate, Hartley Shawcross[,] had in the meantime dropped out of the running). In the end I think the P.M. did the only possible thing in appointing Herbert. The Foreign Secretary ought to be one of the leading figures in the Cabinet & the Party, & within that group the choice has become very small. Person-ally I have no doubt that Nye was the right choice, but that was out of the question in view of his relations with Herbert & Ernie (and to a lesser extent the PM). His reputation in the country (outside the Labour movement) and in [the] USA would probably be also held against him, but personally I do not think that aspect is important.

Anyway it's Herbert we've got. I prefer him to Hector or Patrick Gordon Walker, and I think he was probably a better appointment than Hartley who is pretty unreliable though an infinitely nicer man than Herbert. My relations with Herbert are negligible. I don't think he likes me but if he finds I am effi-cient, he will probably be quite happy to have me where I am – anyway for a while.

He is probably more ignorant of foreign affairs than any other member of the Cabinet. In recent years he has kept out of it, so as not to cross Ernie, & has taken no part. The few interventions I have heard him make in Cabinet have been appalling. Basically he is a little Englander who suspects every-one who is foreign. If he had the power he would like to be a Palmerston.[67] That is not a possible role for a British foreign secretary today, but he may nevertheless try it in a small way, for instance in the Middle East.

He is of course a very clever political tactician, & has his eye on the House of Commons & the polls in a way that Ernie never had. He will there-fore probably be very adroit in small ways & will succeed in building himself up both at home and abroad. This will be quite a good thing. Once he has done that, however, there is no saying how he will use his influence. I fear his influence on British policy if he stays long enough to exert it. I think however that he may want to be firmer with the US, & to make more use of public relations in dealing with them than Ernie did. That, in itself, would be good.

So far I have got a fairly good impression of his attitude & competence. Nevertheless I feel a basic distrust of him & his motives. Moreover he cheapens everything he touches. I think it would be as well if he did not have too long a tenure of this office.

. . . When the changes occurred I was glad to shed some of the respons-ibility. The last two months have been a very big strain. I have been in an impossible position, with far too much work and too little authority. I was aware that the work was not really getting done as it should be, & that was more wearing than everything else. I think I did as well as could be expected, but the whole set-up was impossible.

I shall of course have a far less interesting time now, & no doubt I shall find it irritating to be out of things after having so much responsibility. On the other hand I hope to have a little more time to think & read & keep in touch with the movement and Grimsby. That is very necessary.

This last year has been worth five years of normal experience. I have had three months leading the UK delegation [to the UN] in New York; & out of the remaining months I have been in charge at all the important moments – Schuman plan; Korean war; first move for German rearmament; & the 'Korean resolution' crisis with the Americans after Xmas. During that time I have been continuously in Cabinet, & I think I have established quite a good position in the government & the party. Now I think it will do me no harm to take rather a back seat for a time.

As a result of this experience I have become rather depressed about the leadership of the movement. Clem Attlee is practical & sensible, but doesn't really make the grade as P.M. He decides too easily and changes his mind again too easily. As a subordinate I never really felt that he was a solid support.

Of the other senior ministers there are very few indeed whose judgement & character I respect – at any rate on international matters. Shinwell is terri-ble, Jowitt & Dalton incalculable & several, such as George Tomlinson, Tom Williams & Chuter [Ede], more or less out of their depth. Hugh Gaitskell & Nye are both formidable in their own way & old Addison is pretty shrewd.

Hector and Gordon Walker are pretty competent, but both over ambitious & very reactionary. Harold Wilson is, I think, good on his own subject. On general matters he does not contribute much. Jim Griffiths, whom I like very much, is a bit disappointing, both on his own colonial job, and on more general topics.

All in all, it is not a very impressive group & it has little internal cohesion. I dare say this is usually the case with governments. The policy depends on two or three strong men. In this respect Stafford Cripps has been a sad loss. With Ernie now largely extinct too there is not much real quality left apart from Nye.

One small thing that seems symptomatic of the curious relationship between colleagues is that throughout this whole year, when I have been carrying a weight that no one in my position ought to be asked to carry, I have not had a single word of encouragement of any kind, either from Clem or from Ernie. When I returned from 3 months in N[ew] Y[ork] Ernie did not even ask me 'How did you get on?', let alone say 'You did fine.' Nor did he say a word when he left the F.O. (Actually, at that point I think he was too spiritually exhausted to think of anything.)

I don't much mind about this, as I have had plenty of kind words from elsewhere. I think, however, that it shows a lack of understanding of the art of leadership which is a bit shocking.

We are now in the Easter recess – a cold, wet, early Easter. Prior to that we had several weeks of late nights and pandemonium in the House [of Commons], due to the Tory wish to have an early election which they feel sure of winning. There certainly is a swing against us just now. It may be less pronounced in a few months. I think therefore that we will probably try to stick out the summer, get the budget through, & then see how things stand.

Readers will note that there is no hint in Younger's diary of any belief that he might succeed Bevin as Foreign Secretary. His name did come up in some of the discussions between senior Cabinet members, only to be dismissed on account of his alleged lack of maturity and/or judgement,[68] but in retrospect it is hard to see that he would have performed any worse than Morrison or most of the other candidates for the post. David Owen, moreover, was appointed Foreign Secretary in 1977 at the age of thirty-eight after only one year as Minister of State – Younger was forty-two in 1951 – and he did not have Younger's wartime and intelligence experience. Nevertheless, the political and social climate of 1977 was very different from that of 1951 and Younger was probably right when he was asked about the possibility by Richard Rose in 1961.

... I was very junior really. There wasn't an awful lot of difference in age between me and some of these other people [who were in the running]. But they'd mostly been prominent in the Labour Party for longer. I doubt whether he [Attlee] much liked any of the people who were immediately available. I always felt he quite liked me, but it's conceivable that he thought the Party might not take me as Foreign Secretary ... [T]oo many old hands in the Party ... would just think me a young whippersnapper. I would not carry the authority in difficult decisions like German re-armament and that sort of thing.[69]

4 The end of the Labour government, April–October 1951

Although Younger had anticipated that Herbert Morrison's appointment as Foreign Secretary would reduce his work load, he found that, in the event, he was working as hard as ever. So much so, in fact, that it was to be six weeks before he wrote the next entry in his diary, which is dated 13 May 1951. The intervening period had seen two significant developments on the British political scene: the death of Ernest Bevin and the resignations of Aneurin Bevan, Harold Wilson and John Freeman.[1]

... Poor old Ernie's death[2] was of course important only in a symbolical sense. He had already faded from the political scene. Most of us felt however that his death marked the end of a stage in the history of the party & the government. He was the last great Trade Union figure from the period of pre-war struggle & there is no one comparable to replace him. Now he is gone, & Stafford Cripps too, the old guard in the Cabinet consists only of the PM & Herbert, (Dalton having largely ceased to count).

Now Nye's resignation[3] has removed the only other figure of stature & though the events which drove him out have gone some way to raise the status of Hugh Gaitskell. Hugh, however, can scarcely have the importance in the movement which Nye has; nor do I expect him, for all his ability, ever to achieve the prestige in the country of Stafford Cripps.

I found Nye's resignation very disturbing, for I had always envisaged that if he broke away, I should probably go with him. In the event, there was really no question of my doing so, so I have merely stayed put, feeling acutely uneasy.

The sequence was that Hugh produced a sensible 'orthodox' rather conservative budget, which earned a good deal of applause, & was generally well received even in most parts of the Labour movement which had expected something very bleak. The budget contained however a clause charging for dentures & spectacles under the [National] Health Service so as to keep the ceiling for the service to £400 million. Nye had let it be known publicly before the budget that he would not remain in a government which imposed such charges.

Nye realised however that this was really too slight a disagreement to justify resignation, so in his resignation speech[4] he said relatively little on teeth & specs, and gave as his main reason the excessive level of the defence programme & the impossibility of realising it in view of the crazy policy of [the] US regarding raw materials. He prophesied great disruption of our civilian economy and cited the health charges as evidence that the government now intend to give way to Tory & American war hysteria & sacrifice the welfare state to rearmament.

This line of argument clearly has quite a strong demagogic appeal in the country, since it brings under one umbrella all pacifists, all anti-Americans, & all who believe in a neutral 3rd force between [the] USA & [the] USSR or else don't believe that the Soviet Union is a genuine danger at all. Most of us have misgivings on some or all of these grounds. Many think the arms programme cannot be fulfilled. This however did not seem to be the moment to resign on the issue, since the defence programme was decided before Christmas (when I was in New York) with no more than moderate protests in the Cabinet from Nye & Harold Wilson.[5]

The truth is that this was not the real reason for the resignation at all. Nye's real reason was his growing sense of frustration at being constantly in a minority in Cabinet on all sorts of issues, & a general feeling that the government is steadily slipping towards the right. I think he was egged on to resignation by Jenny, who has long had a sort of political death-urge. I think he was also partly driven out by deliberate intransigence on the part of both Herbert Morrison who was acting Prime Minister and Hugh Gaitskell. I believe that if Attlee, who was in hospital, had been in charge, he might have found some compromise between the two sides.

It is much too early to say what the effect of all this will be. One cannot help thinking that Nye's instinct about the government is largely sound. I would say that Attlee is now the most radical member of it! Moreover (as I noted ten pages or so back)[6] it has clearly lost its impetus. For some time past Pat [Llewellyn-Davies] & I in our frequent discussions have been asking ourselves whether Nye is making a serious attempt to thrash out a new radical line, or whether he is content merely to emit thunder on the left, & we have always agreed that there is no sign of his having attempted to organise either a group of supporters or a line of policy. I think his handling of his resignation confirms this. During the whole episode he seems to have made no attempt to gain support, & indeed in the end he seems to have contemplated resigning alone. He tried to discourage the other two. He was not in touch with old friends like George Strauss, though George had taken a stronger line over the defence programme last December than anyone & in fact had been disappointed at the lack of firmness of both Nye & Harold [Wilson], (both of whom were in the Cabinet which he is not).

Altogether it has been a rather distressing affair, showing Nye at his least impressive. Nevertheless, I still think that he overtops all possible rivals as a future leader. If, in the end, he is kept out of leadership, I think it will be by some group of mediocrities, of whom the best will probably be Gaitskell, Gordon Walker & McNeil.

I think in fact he may very well easily recover the lost ground. Whether he does so or not will depend largely on whether, in the next few months, he proves capable of showing the party that there is a better path to follow than the mere 'consolidation' of Herbert M[orrison] & others.

I only managed to have one serious talk to him before his resignation & have not had one since. John Freeman advised me that he was in a very emotional state & that I would do better to wait till he had had a holiday.

On re-reading this entry in his diary in December 1952, Younger recalled that this 'one serious talk' he had with Bevan, had taken place a couple of days before the latter's resignation. He inserted the following account of that conversation into the diary:

> ... I put it to him that 'teeth & specs', however important to him person-ally, was scarcely an important enough issue to justify the resignation of a potential future party leader like himself. I said 'if you do resign, you really will have to find some way of broadening the issue, otherwise the whole thing will seem rather trivial.' He replied: 'Oh I'll broaden it all right.' But even then he didn't say he was going to make excessive rearmament his main complaint.
>
> In the same conversation I asked him whether he wanted others to resign with him. I said that I did not think he ought to resign at all unless he thought the issue grave enough to justify his trying to rally support for his point of view. I also told him that I had always thought of myself as being in tune with him rather than with the older leaders, but that it was really impossible for people such as myself to follow him on the issue as he had so far presented it. He then said he was not in fact urging others to resign, and was trying to persuade Harold Wilson to stay in office ...

The original diary entry of 13 May 1951 now resumes.

In the meantime I have nothing much new to add about Herbert as Foreign Secretary or my relations with him. What with being acting PM & then having the Festival of Britain opening (always a special interest of his)[7] he has not yet got down to the job. His handling of it, though fairly adroit[,] has been thoroughly superficial, and even the House [of Commons] has begun to notice how ignorant he is every time he answers questions.

I have found him irritating for these reasons, but am still prepared to be convinced that he will turn out all right. The next few weeks will show ...

It was another six weeks before Younger found time to make a further entry in his diary. By then further difficulties had arisen to plague the government. Most important was the dispute between Britain and the

Iranian government over the nationalisation of the Anglo-Iranian Oil Company on 2 May 1951. This remained unsettled when the Labour government lost office in October. Then there was the defection, announced on 7 June 1951, of two Foreign Office officials, Guy Burgess and Donald Maclean, to the Soviet Union. Finally, there was the question of a peace treaty with Japan, the prospect of which aroused similar feelings in Britain to those which were engendered by German rearmament and which were rooted in the same reluctance to allow an ex-enemy and potential commercial rival back into the international community at what was thought to be the insistence of the United States. Younger dealt with all these issues in his diary entry of 24 June 1951.

... [W]e have had (& still have) a major crisis on our hands over Persian[8] Oil. At the present moment it looks like being either a major disaster (if we get driven out altogether) or a minor one if we manage, on rather humiliating terms, to keep the oil flowing. I do not think Herbert has handled things well. He was slow in conceding the principle of nationalisation. Then he hankered after strong-arm methods though it was pretty clear that they couldn't be adopted. The day-to-day business has, I think, been well handled by the office & the Ambassador [in Teheran, Sir Francis] Shepherd, but the over-all strategy has been fumbling. Moreover Herbert does not seem capable of carrying the Cabinet with him & the meetings usually end in some muddled compromise which has to be put right at the next meeting. This week we ended with a debate on Persia.[9] He [Morrison] was the only government speaker and wound up in a rather cheap partisan way which infuriated the Tories & dismayed his own side. At one point the Tory, Legge-Bourke,[10] tossed him a penny & told him to 'put on a new record'.

The Speaker made L[egge]-B[ourke] leave the Chamber, but the gesture was not wholly unsuccessful because it dramatised the low level to which Herbert had already reduced the debate.[11] I think it will take Herbert some time to live all this down.

My own relations with him are, I think[,] good so far. In many small ways he is excellent, and easy to work with. The trouble is that he is proving to be just what I feared – a party politician, out of his depth in questions requiring statesmanship & a sense of history & world forces.

During these weeks Ernest Davies has remained in Paris (his conference[12] has just broken up now without agreement) & I have had to do quite a lot of minor work of his, and of course all the P[arliamentary] Q[uestion]s. The trickiest have been some arising out of the extraordinary incident of the disappearance of Guy Burgess & Donald Maclean, both of [the] F.O., who have not been heard of since leaving for France on 25th May. Though the whole thing is still a mystery, the general assumption is that they may eventually turn up in Soviet-controlled territory. The Tories, knowing that Guy at least has expressed left-wing views in the past, are trying to make political capital out of it & some are calling for a witch hunt on the US model. I have had to answer quite a few questions on this[13] and so far I think I have managed to give nothing away.

Younger's reference to having given nothing away is intriguing. How much more did this former member of MI5 know than he confided to his diary? There is an assertion in one of the many books on the two spies that Guy Burgess, who had just been recalled from the British Embassy in Washington on account of his turbulent private life, had written a long critique of American foreign policy which the British ambassador refused to send to the Foreign Office and which Burgess intended to submit to Younger personally.[14] Whether this document actually existed and, if so, whether Younger ever saw it, we do not know.

Burgess and Maclean had indeed gone to 'Soviet-controlled territory' – Moscow, to be precise – and they remained in the Soviet Union until their deaths in 1963 and 1983 respectively. Both, but especially Maclean, had provided their hosts with a great deal of valuable intelligence over many years and the repercussions of their defection, which came on top of the arrest of the 'atom spy', Klaus Fuchs, in London in February 1950, were considerable, not least in the United States. Nor, of course, were Burgess and Maclean the last such 'moles' to be unearthed.

The diary entry of 24 June 1951 continues:

My main job, however, has been some ten days of talks with John Foster Dulles on the Japanese Peace Treaty.[15] I did not really enjoy it, and had not had as much time to brief myself as I should have liked, and had to put myself very much in the hands of the officials. Actually our Far Eastern officials are, I think, very good, & I trust them. The best of them, Rob Scott[,] was not personally involved in these talks, but Dening[16] and Johnston[17] were both excellent.

Dulles was most reasonable & cooperative, & in the end we got agreement on a draft treaty. I think we will have trouble over it in a number of quarters when it is published, but personally I think that, given the situation in the Far East today, it is a reasonable document. It avoids the issue of who should represent China altogether by not inviting either Chiang or Peking to sign. This is of course unsatisfactory, but inevitable if there is to be any treaty at all.

There will also be criticisms because the treaty will leave Japan free both commercially and militarily. The truth is however that a satisfactory development of Japanese policy depends above all on Japanese–US cooperation & not on restrictive clauses in the treaty. Dulles has constantly emphasised, and I agree with him, that we must not make the mistake of letting Japan become strong again, while inflicting enough pin pricks to stimulate nationalist resentment against us. This was the mistake of Versailles[18] & I agree that we should not repeat it.

On Korea, there is news today (on the anniversary of the aggression) that

Malik[19] has made a UN broadcast in N[ew] Y[ork] calling for a cease-fire. This just *may* be the chance we have been waiting for to end what will otherwise be a long & costly stalemate.

I was made a Privy Councillor in the [King's] Birthday Honours list.[20] Most if not all of my predecessors as Minister of State have been made PCs on appointment. I had thought I might get it at [the] New Year, after the General Assembly, so I was glad to have it now. I really think I earned it.

... During this period there have been no developments in the 'Nye Bevan' controversy. There is a pamphlet just due to come out which may give a clue as to what he is thinking.[21] There is little indication that he has any very precise programme in mind.

The next entry in Younger's diary was dated 22 July 1951.

This last month has been taken up with the same main issues – Korea & Persia. In Korea military armistice talks are now going on.[22] It looks as though the Russians at least want an end to the fighting; presumably the Chinese have agreed, though I am not so sure that they are really keen. They may pitch their terms higher than the Russians, because they have more interest in Korea itself. So far as the Russians are concerned I suspect this recent move is part of a big attempt to slow down western rearmament, perhaps with a special eye on the Japanese Peace Treaty & the possibility of Japanese rearmament. (The Russians are stepping up their peace campaign generally & have just issued a new periodical 'News' for promoting friendship between the Russian & British peoples).

All this is encouraging in that it shows that the Russians are not in a mood to heighten the conflict or even start a larger war before American rearmament gets going. I think Russia has been cautious at all points ever since the UN decision to resist in Korea took them by surprise. I never have believed that the Russians would deliberately court a world war, & it is quite likely that they now realise that their stupidity has promoted a vast rearmament in the west, & they had better try to put the whole process into reverse. They have left it very late to do so, with the result that everyone (especially the Americans) treats every friendly move with deep suspicion. It is certainly too early to rush to conclusions about any major change of policy, but many people (including many ministers) seem to me to be going much too far in suggesting that practically no Soviet action can be allowed to slow up our own rearmament. I think if the Korean negotiations succeed, there *will* be some slowing up anyway, though we have not yet reached the point where we can be content with our own strength.

This subject has become exceedingly topical owing to the publication of a 'Tribune' pamphlet, prefaced by Nye Bevan, Harold Wilson & John Freeman, called 'One Way Only'.[23] The theme of this is broadly that the strength of the Soviet Union has been greatly overestimated; that our own arms programme, designed to spend £4,700 m. in 3 years, is therefore far larger than is needed, and is in any case larger than we can carry without serious damage to our living standards & our ability to contribute to the development of backward areas. Present policy, therefore, it is argued, is likely to cause the west to lose the contest with communism on the civilian front, through its undue preoccupation with military defence. Other sections of the pamphlet deal with the rising cost of living (due largely to world rearmament) and the domestic measures to be taken to meet it, but the main theme is excessive rearmament, alleged to be due to submissiveness to the Americans.

I find myself in general agreement with many things in the pamphlet, but I do not really think that the data in it sustain the conclusion that we have to make fundamental changes of policy. Admittedly there is a considerable difference of emphasis & of background thinking between the writers & the government, but they do not really face the question of *how much* rearmament ought to go on. I don't think they have made up their minds themselves. There are of course many of us in the government who are in the same state. *I* am sure that our 3 year programme is excessive, and will not in fact be needed; *I* think the Russian threat is probably overestimated. But I think there *is* a threat, that we need higher levels of armament than we have at the moment, and that the way to secure adjustments over the next couple of years is to stay in the government and work to that end. I believe Nye & Harold could have been quite effective if they had done so. Now however they are being forced to make out that they differ in *principle* & not merely in degree from the government. In order to do this they find themselves using arguments very near to the communist line, with which they certainly are not in agreement, & this makes them highly vulnerable to criticism. I am very much afraid that Herbert will see his chance to crush Nye completely in the National Executive[24] & at the Party Conference in the autumn. I do not think the victory will necessarily be very long-lived, but if there is no compromise on either side, morale in the party will be seriously damaged in the constituencies, however big the votes at conference may be.

The only hope of this being avoided is the P.M. I should think he would make an effort to hold Herbert back, especially as I get the impression that there is at present little love lost between the P.M. & Herbert.

Herbert has not been doing very well at the F.O. in recent weeks, & still gives an impression of ignorance & superficiality. On Persia, and indeed on other important matters[,] it is the P.M. and the Cabinet who decide things. Herbert makes very bold, fierce noises which have no substance behind them. I still get on quite well with him on a day-to-day basis, & indeed I find him good to work with in a way, but basically I have no confidence in him at all, & my respect for him is not increasing.

We still do not know whether the Persian crisis will be solved or not. Aver[ell] Harriman[25] is in Teheran now. If he does not produce any results within a week or so from now, it looks as though we will be forced out of the oilfields, at least for the time being. If that should occur, it will be pretty damaging to British prestige, & of course also to the government, & to Herbert in particular. At the present moment that is important domestically, because many people want an autumn election on the assumption that a Korean truce and a Persian settlement will raise the government's stock enough to give us a real chance of winning. If Persia went wrong the whole calculation would be upset.

Averell Harriman had arrived in Teheran on 15 July 1951. According to Dean Acheson the decision to send him arose from the Anglo-Iranian Oil Company's threat to shut down operations, which Acheson feared might lead to 'an economic collapse in Iran, a Communist coup and loss of Iranian oil to the West'. There was also the possibility that if the British intervened militarily to protect the AIOC's staff and refinery at Abadan on the Persian Gulf, as they were hinting they might, the Russians would probably move into the north Iranian province of Azerbaijan, as they had sought to do in 1945–6. Harriman's mission was designed to prevent these horrendous possibilities from materialising by persuading the British and the Iranians to resume negotiations which had earlier broken down.[26]

The diary entry of 22 July 1951 continues:

I am not convinced that the P.M. will want an autumn election, & I wouldn't mind betting that Herbert won't. He will see too much danger from Nye in the event of a Labour defeat. The P.M. will probably be influenced above all by the need to keep the party united. If the only way to close the ranks is to have an autumn election, then I expect he will do it.

A foreign affairs debate took place in the House of Commons on 25 July 1951,[27] which as Younger explained in his next diary entry, dated 6 August 1951, dealt mainly with the recently published draft Japanese Peace Treaty.[28]

... The criticisms were mainly of the dangers of renewed [Japanese] competition – quite justifiable fears, but not matters which could be dealt with in the treaty. Apart from the unavoidable necessity of leaving China out of the treaty (owing to the disagreement about which is the legal gov[ernmen]t of China) I am really fairly satisfied that this treaty is as good as could be expected. It is quite clear that the USSR would not agree to any treaty which would give any reasonable assurances to us or [the] U.S. of Japanese cooperation, & she will obviously do her best to make Japan communist & drive out American influence. She may succeed in the long run. But however that may be, I do not think anything we could have done at this stage would have offered the slightest hope of Far Eastern collaboration with her, so I am sure we have been right to go ahead to try to get a peace of some sort. We may yet have trouble before signature in

September,[29] but I think it will go through, with the great majority of interested nations participating . . .

After a visit to Geneva to lead the British delegation to the UN Economic and Social Committee at the end of July, Younger took a week's holiday from 6 to 12 August 1951. On his return he found himself once more in charge at the Foreign Office for a fortnight. His next diary entry, which is dated 28 August 1951, takes up the story.

. . . I was pretty busy, but not overworked, because there were no Cabinets & the House [of Commons] was in recess. Dick Stokes[30] was leading a mission in Teheran, so that the day-to-day work on the oil dispute was considerably reduced. He has now suspended the talks & returned home, & we still don't know what the outcome is going to be. Personally I am not expecting a favourable outcome. It seems to me unlikely that the Persians dare agree to any terms which the British staff [of the AIOC] would accept. That is really the limiting factor in the generosity which it is possible for us to show. It would not be much good for us to satisfy Musaddiq,[31] if as a result all the British staff walked out & the oil came to a standstill anyway. No oil has been flowing for some weeks now. All our people are out of the oil fields & only a nucleus is left at Abadan. It looks therefore as if we have at last reached the point when Persian workers will not get paid & there will be unemployment and discontent. No one seems to have much idea how this situation will develop – whether towards a communist coup, or to strong action by the Shah[32] (who is not at all a strong man but is said to have the loyalty of the army). If the former seems probable I should expect the Americans to be prepared to sacrifice the British oil interests in order to prevent it, e.g. by helping the Persians to restart the oil flow without our participation. I can't honestly say that this would be a wholly unreasonable attitude for an American to take, but it could cause great tension between us & [the] U.S. [The] U.S. are not at all good at backing us up & it is only quite recently that they have done so in this dispute. Even now Harriman has, I think, left his way open to 'write off' the Anglo-Iranian interest and save Persia from the communists.

I have for many weeks past had the feeling of standing right outside this particular affair, & I don't feel involved in it. My own summing up would be that our last chances of a really suitable settlement went when Musaddiq got into power.[33] Before that, I think a more imaginative policy would have enabled his predecessor to settle the whole thing. Since then there has been no common ground, & now Musaddiq risks assassination if he makes further concessions to us. I doubt whether any other minister could act otherwise unless the Shah were to sponsor a strong-hand government which would imprison the main 'agitators' & virtually rule by decree for a time. I am very doubtful whether he will do this. In any case the whole British position in Persia is bound to be, at best, most precarious in the future.

I think we have largely brought this upon ourselves by allowing a private company free rein to make enormous profits without considering longterm national policy, despite H[is] M[ajesty's] G[overnment] having 51% of the shares & two government directors on the board. I have put up a minute to Herbert on this with a view to forestalling a recurrence of this sort of thing elsewhere in the world, but so far I have had no response.

In his minute, which was dated 3 July 1951, Younger referred in particular to possible problems in both Burma and Iraq, and expressed the view that the government could not afford to leave it to the oil companies involved to anticipate trouble ahead.[34] Although we know that some action was taken as a result of this minute,[35] we do not know the details as the relevant Foreign Office file seems to have been destroyed.

The diary entry of 28 August 1951 continues:

Most other issues, such as the Korean cease-fire talks, which are in suspense, have remained more or less static through this holiday period. Diplomatic activity is just about to restart on a big scale. The whole question of German rearmament will be reopened at the Atlantic Council in mid-Sept[ember] (our Cabinet still being divided on this); and even before that the threatened trouble over the Japanese Peace Treaty is going to come to a head at San Francisco. The USSR is coming to the conference with proposals which are not revealed, but are virtually certain to have as their object the scrapping of the present draft & the linking of the treaty with the Far Eastern problem as a whole.

Owing to Herbert being unwilling to cut short his holiday in order to be at the start of the conference, I am going to head the [British] delegation until he arrives. We will have a small but strong delegation including Oliver Franks & Rob Scott. It should be most interesting, but rather worrying. It is not impossible that the Russians may get quite strong support for the view that this treaty, by by-passing China, is going to raise tension & prejudice eventual settlement in the Far East. Asian countries in particular may feel this. The Russians may link the treaty with the possibility of ending the Korean war, & there may be some response to this here & in Europe.

While I propose to keep a somewhat open mind until I see what the Soviet proposals actually are, my present feeling is that this last minute intervention by the Soviet[s], after 11 months of obstruction or silence, is most unlikely to be sincerely meant as a step to peace. I think its purpose will be wholly disruptive, & its main intention to prevent the U.S. from putting its relations with Japan on a stable & permanent basis.

So far as we are concerned, whatever our misgivings, I think we have to rely on the U.S. to handle the Japanese problem, since clearly we cannot spare a man or a gun to share in Japanese defence or to prevent Japan from becoming once more aggressive. We cannot therefore share the

Soviet/Chinese view that the Americans should get out of the Far East (and even if [the] UK could, Australia & N[ew] Z[ealand] most certainly wouldn't). Therefore we can do no other than support the U.S. in pushing through the present treaty – as they will almost certainly wish to do.

I don't much like the role myself, & I think it may get a bad press at home, but I see no alternative at present.

The San Francisco trip has lopped two weeks off my three weeks' holiday! I am now having the remaining week, before flying to S[an] F[rancisco] in 4 days time . . .

Just before going on holiday I took part in two 'schools' on international affairs[36] . . . It was hard work, but I enjoyed it & was able to get a fairly clear impression of the main things that are bothering labour people.

The real difficulty for most people is to accept that there is a real threat from [the] USSR. This is quite natural in view of past history, and the position is not helped by the exaggeration of the Russian menace which is so widespread just now & merely increases the suspicion that the whole thing is simply a Tory ramp for which the Labour leaders have fallen.

Nearly all the other difficulties flow from this – the fear that the Americans are the real aggressive force, the conviction that German rearmament is both risky (which most people would agree upon) and unnecessary, and that our rearmament if not unnecessary is at any rate excessive.

Every time I meet these objections, I search my conscience to see whether they have any substance. One would so like to believe them if one could. I always reach the conclusion that, whatever my misgivings, on all these points (and they are considerable), I could not take the responsibility of following a policy which did not provide against the possibility of Soviet expansion, both in Europe & the east, promoted by a mixture of subversion & armed threat. Even where one would wish to support revolutionary forces, Soviet policy makes it virtually impossible to do so, because it follows up social revolution in any country by tying that country to the Soviet Union & cutting it off from the rest of the world. One has seen this in eastern Europe. In China we have been trying to prevent the same process from developing, but the prospects of success are getting rather dim, & it seems more & more likely that we shall have to regard Chinese expansion as a danger in the next few years.

To blame US policy for the deterioration in the Far East is not unreasonable, provided one doesn't pretend they are solely to blame. But it doesn't alter the power problem which we have to face – a militant aggressive Soviet/Chinese combination which is not prepared to cooperate with us & is seeking to damage us wherever it can. In a struggle of that kind one must either give up or organise the maximum strength on one's own side. That is why the US alliance is indispensable to us, and that is what most of the critics won't face. Admittedly it isn't a pleasant thing to have to face, but I don't see how people in positions of authority can avoid it.

At [one school], the main problem was German rearmament. I see all the dangers of it, but I didn't find that the arguments put forward shook my conviction that some German defence contribution in the more or less early future is inevitable. The only room for choice lies in the timing and conditions. Unfortunately Herbert M[orrison] seems to take the American view that there is great urgency and that the conditions do not greatly matter. That is not the general Cabinet view, but the Cabinet is so muddled & indecisive on this subject as to be quite ineffective.

During this last year I have had so much to do that I feel badly in need of a period for digestion of these great issues. It doesn't look as if I will get it now so long as this Parliament lasts.

When he wrote the next entry in his diary, which is dated 9 September 1951, Younger was on a plane returning from San Francisco. The conference on the Japanese Peace Treaty, which was attended by representatives of forty-eight countries, had begun on the evening of 4 September and ended with the signature of the treaty on the morning of the 8th.[37] As Younger records,

... That was the precise timetable which had been planned at the outset when it was thought very unlikely that the Russians would be there. Once we knew Gromyko[38] was coming, few of us really thought that the schedule could be maintained – at any rate not without an indecent amount of 'rail-roading' by the majority & by the chair. In the event, Gromyko put up a half-hearted performance, Acheson did very well in the chair, & the whole thing went without a hitch. So far so good. Just *how* far it takes us is quite another matter.

... [Ours] was a very strong team. I wish I had as much confidence in other sections of the office as I have in this bunch who deal with the Far East. I find them as convincing as I find the Middle Eastern people unconvincing.

Oliver Franks [also] is a tower of strength. Although I saw him last autumn, I had never really worked with him until this week. Intellectually he is most formidable & has an astonishing grasp of the basic factors in all the problems with which he is concerned, i.e. at the moment all the problems which we habitually discuss with the Americans. He is reputed to be Olympian and alarming. There is an element of this, but I think it is quite unintentional. So far as I am concerned, any feeling of alarm is merely due to the sense that if one says anything wild, or based on superficial judgements it will be promptly punctured! I felt somewhat awkward at first, because he had originally been named to lead the delegation until Herbert Morrison arrived at the end of the week, & then I came in over his head. I am however quite satisfied that there was no petty ill-feeling on his side. I gather he holds the view that on all big occasions the people with the political responsibility ought to lead, & he thinks it a great weakness in the American system that, with the exception of the president himself, none of the U.S. cabinet have a popular vote at their backs & all of them are simply appointees.

... We had a day & a half before the conference began, & spent it contacting other delegations, especially the Commonwealth and the Americans. The main worry was the rules of procedure. There had been much speculation about the motives of the Russians in attending the conference. None of us were clear about this, but it seemed pretty certain that they would wish to start a number of new hares running, and would not accept our view that this was a conference called simply to comment on and sign a treaty whose text had already been negotiated through diplomatic channels. Our problem was therefore to draw the rules of procedure tight enough to prevent filibustering, while at the same time preserving the decencies of debate & securing the widest possible support for the methods employed. On the whole we managed this fairly well.

Truman made a good speech[39] – pretty uncompromising on the defence issue, but nevertheless definitely a 'pacific' speech with no concessions to the warmongering sections of US opinion ... Afterwards there was a big reception. The only item of interest was that when the chief delegates lined up to meet the President I was next [to] Gromyko. He was most affable, but clearly disinclined to talk seriously. He remarked that he thought we might be here a month! I took this as little more than a jocular feeler to get my reaction. The press however got hold of it, & wrote it up into quite a story of forthcoming Soviet obstruction.

On the Wednesday[40] we debated the rules of procedure, & to our great surprise got it finished by lunch time. It is true that this was due to a closure motion by the Latin [American] bloc, (which the US had made every effort to prevent), but in fact the debate was dying on its feet before the closure motion was put. Gromyko, backed by the Poles (Wierblowski)[41] and the Czechs (Mme. Sekaninova[,])[42] put up a most perfunctory opposition & missed several good chances. Gromyko does not usually miss chances, especially on procedure, and most of us concluded that he was not seriously trying.

I was involved in a trifling incident which earned me a lot of limelight. I was called to the rostrum on a point of order, following Wierblowski whom Acheson had ruled out of order. W[ierblowski] protested & would not leave the rostrum, & for a time he & I were side by side under the television arc lamps. Eventually he went away, & I of course had been careful not to push him off or otherwise create a scene. The press commentators & television, however, were intent on turning the whole episode into a gladiatorial spectacle, & tried to make the incident into a drama.[43]

The main debate was opened by the two sponsors, Dulles speaking first and I second. My speech was a product of many hands and was not my own at all. It was not an exciting speech, but a good steady effort for the record. It seemed to go down quite well and got a good press.[44]

Gromyko & his colleagues made more or less common form propaganda speeches, picking up all the obvious points, such as the absence of the Chinese & Indians, the military tie up with [the] U.S. etc.[,] but not ramming them home with any great force, or saying anything which was particularly embarrassing. In view of the many weakish points in our case, & the mis-givings felt in many countries, I thought the Soviet performance very mediocre. Gromyko ended with a series of amendments which would in effect have made an entirely different treaty. I don't suppose he ever expected them to be formally considered as amendments, & the president ruled them out of order, quite rightly, on the ground that the invitation issued was to conclude a treaty on the basis of the existing draft text. In any case, the proposals seemed to me unacceptable not merely to those who wish to see [the] U.S. granted military facilities in Japan, but also to nearly all, including the Asians, who favour a liberal treaty.

It was an odd performance, and I really don't know to whom the Soviet proposals were expected to appeal. Only, I think, to the Chinese commu-nists. Perhaps that is sufficient explanation.

The rest of the debate was flat, despite several good speeches. Yoshida [Shigeru], the P.M. of Japan[,] ended the main debate with a stereotyped somewhat aggressive speech, obviously designed for the Japanese public, with one or two consolation prizes for the Americans & nothing for anyone else![45]

About 3 hours were then given for further statements. Gromyko spoke again, saying nothing new, & consequently Dulles & I felt that we must reply. I spoke for some 15 minutes, more or less impromptu, & was, I think, rather a success.[46] Once again, however, I got involved in a comic turn, because when I had been speaking a few minutes Gromyko & some of his associates got up and went out, followed by the Poles & Czechs. Immedi-ately the public galleries went wild and all the commentators became madly excited (and very noisy), thinking this was the big walk out. I had to stop speaking several times to let the noise subside, while Acheson vainly ham-mered for order.

Some five minutes later the scene became hilarious when Gromyko & his friends came stalking back & resumed their seats! Again I had to stop. Fortunately I was not attempting to stir emotion, so the interruption did not upset me at all.[47]

This episode high-lighted what has been one of the striking features of the week. Radio & television has taken charge in this country to a fantastic extent, and applies all its news-sense & gift for sensationalism to making politics a melodrama, and politicians film stars. The public being very naif & enthusiastic got to the point of wanting to kill the Russians, & madly cheer-ing everyone who slanged Soviet policy. My own two interventions were perfectly adequate but quite undramatic. While I naturally attacked Gromyko's proposals I used no picturesque phrases, let alone abuse. Yet the day after the conference when I went shopping I found that almost liter-ally everyone in S[an] F[rancisco] knew me – every girl behind the counter, people on the pavements & in restaurants – and a very large number came up & shook my hand off, & said gee I was fine, and I sure gave those SOBs the works!

It was an astonishing experience for me – exhilarating up to a point, but soon becoming rather a bore, especially as I was quite well aware that I had said nothing which would have earned even a sentence of comment at home.

The most interesting by-product of all this was its effect on Dean Acheson's position. He has now been violently slandered for two years. He is not personally well-known on the west coast, where few people have ever seen him. In consequence most people think of him as a Soviet agent, a 'toff', and a fool. During this week, when he was in the chair at all crucial times, he was seen & heard at work by a public which at the peak of the conference is said to have numbered 27 millions! He was seen to stand up to Gromyko, and to be 'smart' on points of order. He was dignified, and ended the conference with an exceedingly well judged speech of about 10 minutes or less, delivered without a note & on the sort of moral–religious level which appeals most to the sort of stupid, sentimental, patriotic American who has been most hostile to him.[48]

Everyone seems to agree that the result of all this has been a personal triumph for Acheson which, for a short time at least, will go a long way to restore him to a position of strength & influence. He himself feels this to be so.

I must say, the whole thing fills one with alarm. Television is a legitimate political instrument which we have barely begun to use as yet in England. But with a public as simple as the American the power of television in a moment of crisis could, I believe, mean the difference between peace & war. Moreover a man of Hitler's talents might sweep the whole country off its feet. When one thinks that this conference was, in essence, a flop from a news point of view as soon as Gromyko had spoken, one can picture the American public's hysteria if there really was a tense contest going on.

Even apart from television the press & radio are in a warmongering mood – noticeably more than in New York before Xmas. Oliver Franks says it was worse six months ago & is just the 'groundswell' of the MacArthur controversy.[49] That doesn't reassure one much!

On a more serious level the conference must certainly be accounted a success. The fact that the Soviets made no impression on any of the Asians present, & that 48 countries, including Indonesia, signed [the treaty] was certainly a diplomatic reverse. The absence of India was of limited significance because it was clear that they would have found the Soviet proposals even less acceptable than the present draft. There was a general sense that the Soviet Union's policy has been steadily driving everyone into firmer opposition to them.

I have spent the week emphasising to the Americans that I do not regard this as a big step forward, nor have I any confidence in future Japanese behaviour. Nevertheless I feel sure the treaty had to be made. The risks of maintaining the occupation any longer would certainly be greater than the risks of bringing it to an end. The treaty was simply something that had to be done. If things go wrong in the Far East, I don't think it will be on account of the treaty. I do not believe that intensified Russian or Chinese activity e.g. in Korea or Indo-China, if it should occur, will have any very close connection with this treaty, although propaganda may well represent that it has.

It is all part of the dilemma in which Soviet policy has landed us. Their strategy of non-cooperation is so uncompromising that we have only the two alternatives of going our own way, disregarding their interests & wishes; or allowing ourselves to be reduced to total frustration. No amount of flexibility on our side is sufficient to secure reasonable progress in partnership with the Soviet Union. We have already learnt this in Trieste,[50] Austria[51] & W[est] Germany & generally in [the] U.N.; & the Japanese problem is similar in principle. In practice however it is different because [the] U.S. has such control in Japan, and action in defiance of Soviet wishes is therefore possible. What is dangerous is that China & Russia are acting as one, and though in the short run it is possible to ignore China, there can be no long-term settlement of the Far Eastern area without her. I think that is something we must never lose sight of. Unfortunately we are not likely to see a realistic U.S. policy on China this side of the Presidential election in Nov[ember] 1952.

... Originally I was not too keen to do this trip, but I am very glad now that I did it. Although I myself know that I did nothing remarkable at all, I think it is a fact that I had quite a considerable personal success. Television had made me overnight quite a well-known figure in [the] U.S. I think it was my youthful appearance compared with nearly all the other delegates as much as anything I said that made me an object of interest.

Herbert Morrison only arrived out for the final ceremony on Saturday,[52] so I led throughout the whole working period of the conference. It was clear from what he said to me that he had been told that I had done well. I think I am by now fairly well proof against the vacuous flattery of these international conferences. The only compliment I valued on this occasion was from Oliver Franks who took the trouble to come to my room to congratulate me on having led the delegation 'with great distinction'.

Ten days after Younger left San Francisco, on 19 September 1951, Prime Minister Attlee announced that the long-awaited General Election would take place on 25 October. What turned out to be the last weeks of the Labour government also witnessed the climax of the Iranian oil crisis. Younger dealt with the latter in the next entry in his diary, which is dated 3 October 1951.

... The Persian affair has been coming to a head, ending with an [Iranian] ultimatum to our last remaining staff in Abadan,[53] who are leaving this week. We are not intervening by armed force, and have appealed to the [UN] Security Council. The Americans are giving us very poor support,[54] and it looks quite possible that we may get something of a rebuff. I have always thought this possible, and am therefore less shocked than many people seem to be, but of course there is no doubt that the blow to our prestige will be serious, especially in the Middle East. It may easily lead to trouble in Egypt.

The role of the Americans in all this is complicated. They have been critical of us all along for not recognising Persian nationalism and giving the Persians a far better deal. They think [the] AIOC's handling of the matter a hangover from British Imperialism. So far I think they are on the whole right. H[is] M[ajesty's] G[overnment] has been let down by the AIOC (and Sir William Fraser[55] in particular) who have been both greedy & short-sighted. As a government, however, we cannot escape responsibility for this, since we hold 51% of the AIOC shares, have two government directors, and could have intervened had we realised how things were going. The main culprits are the Treasury who appointed the directors, but never expected them to do a real job, & certainly never expected them to keep an eye on political developments in Persia. Maybe the Treasury would say that that was the Embassy's job. That is not a complete answer, but it certainly is the case that the Embassy gave us no advance warning; and that since the dispute began, they have consistently underestimated the force of Persian nationalism and have prophesied the fall of Mussadiq far too readily.

In all this the Americans have been more right than we (which is galling) but they have also been most indiscreet and even hostile in their tactical handling of the whole situation. It is at least arguable that but for encouragement from certain Americans (especially the Ambassador [Henry] Grady) the Persians would long since have made terms with us.

There is also doubt about the role of American oil companies. I have seen no evidence of sinister activity on their part myself, but some allege that they are paying some of the worst Persian agitators, and that their aim is to complete their world oil monopoly by replacing us in Abadan. This would be perfectly logical, & incidentally in line with what a Marxist would expect – imperialist rivalry etc. – but I doubt myself if there is much substance in it. It may be that the oil companies, without positively trying to squeeze us out[,] are making their dispositions for cashing in in the event of our getting squeezed out anyway.

Whatever the various motives, I think the position now is that the Americans will think almost exclusively of preserving stability in Persia, and scarcely at all about saving British assets or British face. If it becomes necessary for the preservation of stability to aid Persia or even to send American technicians, I do not see why they should refrain from doing so.

Their effect upon opinion here could be pretty bad, but there would be little we could do about it.

It is really a very lamentable story in which the blame is shared by many. I cannot wholly escape, since the supplemental oil agreement[56] did come to my notice in [the] summer of 1950[57] & I did not see the dangers of the trend that was developing. I don't however feel much guilt because I was so grossly overworked then, was without a foreign secretary, and was then absent on leave and at [the] UN for four months, by which time the situation had already gone pretty far.

Philip N[oel]-B[aker] is the only minister who has a really clean record in the matter, having poured out warnings at least since January.[58] Nye did the same in about Jan[uary] or Feb[ruary], but nothing effective was done about it. This was one of the consequences of Ernie [Bevin] being half-dead for the whole of his last year.

Since Herbert became Foreign Secretary, and especially in recent weeks, this affair has cast a pretty clear and unattractive light upon the political sagacity & instincts of a number of my colleagues in the government. Several of them have approached the whole affair in a purely emotional way, and have wanted 'strong action', i.e. a military expedition to seize and hold Abadan. Herbert himself has been in the forefront of this group, and the silliest, with Jowitt & A.V. Alexander[59] following closely behind him. Shinwell, though more or less unintelligible, appeared to be somewhat of the same way of thinking, but was even more futile, putting all his faith apparently in breaking off diplomatic relations. Fortunately the P.M. was backed by most others in a sounder view.

What shocked me in a way even more was that Roger Makins, deputising for the absent Strang, also recommended the use of force. When I spoke to him he did not seem to have made any effort at all to think out the consequences. He thought there would be a row at [the] UN which would blow over (that might be correct). But when I asked what he thought would happen in Persia he was merely futile. He appeared to foresee not a capitulation to us, but a consolidation of extremists with the Shah going into exile. He could not answer my question what we should do if our troops in Abadan were shelled or bombed from the mainland. In short he talked like one of the less responsible Tory back benchers. That an official of his standing & repute should be prepared to recommend on the strength of such half-baked thinking that we should take military action in breach of the [UN] Charter & in face of American opposition seems to me staggering. It very much lowers him in my estimation & almost makes me rule him out as a suitable P[ermanent] U[nder] S[ecretary] of the future.

I never had to argue my view because it was not asked for, & when I attended the final cabinet it was clear that Herbert would be overruled in any case. I have never felt so strongly as I did at that meeting that the Cabinet is a body with no common basis to its thinking and that it is quite unequal to big decisions. It was a depressing experience.[60]

I do not think I could serve much longer under Herbert. He is ignorant, amateurish, cheap & reactionary. He is only saved from total disaster by the fact that, on the whole, he accepts the official view which is both more intelligent & less reactionary than his own. When (as on this occasion) the office goes wrong, Herbert plunges in wholeheartedly after it . . .

On the following day, 4 October 1951, Younger added what he called 'a postscript' to the story.

. . . I met Mountbatten[61] tonight at the French Embassy and he told me of a whole series of letters he had written in early April to Herbert, as well as an interview with him, urging a high level ministerial mission to Persia to welcome oil nationalisation & get alongside the Persians to help in carrying it out. Mountbatten said that he thought he had convinced Herbert on two occasions, but when he later saw the [Cabinet] defence committee minutes he was dismayed to find that his views had not even been mentioned. I presume Herbert had in the meantime been swung around by advice in the office. As far as I could make out from Mountbatten, the crucial period occurred when Attlee was in hospital & Herbert, very new in his job, was mainly engaged in forcing Nye's resignation. At that time there was of course in effect no Foreign Secretary at all, and the moment was missed. Perhaps it was already too late, since it was after Rasmara's murder,[62] but Mountbatten thinks there was still time then. Anyway, it was the last moment at which the present debacle might have been prevented.[63]

The tragedy of the whole thing is that, though we are mainly blamed for lack of 'firmness', our real sin is to have followed a reactionary Tory type of policy, getting bad advice both from [the] Anglo-Iranian [Oil Company], to whom we allowed far too much power, and from our Embassy. It is incidentally a serious reflection on the Embassy that when it really became necessary to have in Teheran experts who could handle a Persian political situation, we had to send out far too late a couple of experts from Oxford [University] who had done S[pecial] O[perations] E[xecutive] work in Persia in the war.[64]

Enlarging upon the diary entries for 3 and 4 October 1951, Younger wrote a long and detailed minute on Iran on the 6th. A small portion of this minute has already been published by Anthony Sampson in his book on the major oil companies,[65] but the full text is printed for the first time as an Appendix to this book.[66] It is a powerful critique of British policy in which no one, including Younger himself, is spared.

The remainder of the diary entry of 4 October 1951 dealt with the Labour Party conference at Scarborough, which took place from 1 to 3 October 1951.

. . . It was curtailed owing to the election, and was really more of a demonstration than a conference. Nye made up his quarrel with the rest of the [National] Executive 'for the duration' & there was then nothing much to be said. Speeches on the whole were anodyne & boring. The only events worth comment were a speech of unusual worthlessness by Herbert at the pre-conference demonstration, which lost him much of his remaining prestige even among the loyalest followers; and the elections to the Constituency posts on the Executive. In these Nye swept into first place followed by Barbara Castle[67] & Tom Driberg[;][68] the only 'Bevanite' not elected was Harold Wilson, and Shinwell was dropped.

Of course it is not unusual for the constituencies to be both leftish and a bit irresponsible. Nevertheless the extent of the Bevanite success and the dropping of the Minister of Defence were matters of some political significance & were felt by the right wing leaders to be quite a slap in the face . . .

The General Election took place on 25 October 1951. Younger slightly increased his own majority in Grimsby from 6,412 in February 1950 to 6,851 in October 1951. Indeed, the Labour Party won slightly more votes than the Conservatives over the country as a whole, but due to the vagaries of the British electoral system, it lost twenty seats in the House of Commons while the Conservatives gained twenty-three. The great post-war Labour government was at an end and the party was not to regain power for thirteen years. Younger commented on the campaign and the result in his diary entry of 29 October 1951.

. . . [During the second week of the campaign] I did a very stimulating three days' tour in the midlands . . .

It was pretty exhausting, but I enjoyed it & came back [to Grimsby] feeling far more full of fight than before. Everywhere I went the spirit of the party was so good and the candidates were working hard & seemed optimistic. Everywhere crowded attentive meetings & limited opposition. Everywhere the Tories were talking rather dishonest rubbish & producing no alternative policy to ours at all. While we had no *new* policy to propound, at least we had a more realistic existing policy. Despite all my misgivings about the effect of a Labour victory upon the party, I came back from the tour feeling I really wanted to win. It was so clear that whatever mistakes Labour had made, the Tories would have made the same only worse. The real mistakes we have made are quite the opposite of what the Tories make out. We have not departed sufficiently far from their policy in a number of respects. The more I heard what they were saying, the less I felt they *deserved* to be entrusted with power . . .

During the whole trip, I never got any sense of a swing against Labour. Our own support seemed solider than ever, & the Tories the same. The whole position seemed set in a rigid mould . . .

[On election night a] long string of 'no change' results in the boroughs, followed by one or two very narrow losses of marginal seats soon made it pretty clear that, although there was practically no swing, the ex-liberal voters were going to put us out.[69]

I didn't feel depressed. I had never thought we could have a large majority; and I had dreaded another parliament with the previous dreary cabinet, which seemed unlikely to be much improved, still less to have any new ideas. I really think it is better that we should be out before our morale & our unity begin to crumble seriously.

Quite apart from the fact that everyone anticipates a very critical financial situation developing shortly, and a pretty hard winter at home, I think the fact is that our government was unlikely to produce any radical solutions for any of the nation's problems. If the policy is to be a conservative one in any case, I think it is better that conservatives *should* carry it out. Better certainly for the labour party, whose function is surely to provide the radical force in British public life. If we were to go on pursuing orthodox & conservative policies, I think it could not be long before some other radical grouping grew up, either by way of breakaway from official labour, or even, eventually, out of the C[ommunist] P[arty].

As things are there is a chance that we may be able to re-think our ideas, get rid of some out-dated slogans, and come forward again with a worthwhile radical programme. I should not be surprised if it took us two parliaments to work out such a programme *and* win an election on it.

Of course outside events may cause crisis & lead to new elections, or even an attempt at coalition, but so far as I can see, there is no reason why this parliament should not go [on] for at least 3 years.

So far as my personal position is concerned, too, I think it is a good thing to be in opposition.

For one thing I am frankly very tired. These last 20 months have been packed with experience, and I have been seriously overworked. I have also had to carry a strain far beyond anything I could normally expect owing to Ernie Bevin's illness & Herbert [Morrison]'s incompetence.

During the whole period, although there have been only a few issues upon which I have seriously disagreed with official policy, that is largely because Attlee has kept things reasonably straight, and has been far more progressive than Ernie or Herbert or many others in his cabinet. Indeed since Herbert became Foreign Secretary, only Attlee has stood between us & the most shocking policies. I think it was high time Herbert's foreign interlude was ended, & defeat may have been the only way to do it.

On more personal grounds, I am even more glad of a change. I have hardly seen my family recently, and all my weekends & evenings at home (which have been all too rare) have been taken up with ploughing through masses of official papers. I have scarcely read a book, or seen a play or film in months, and I have seen very few of my friends outside politics. All this would, I am sure, be very bad if it went on for long. Already I feel rather out of touch with ordinary life, and I feel my outlook narrowing. I can't allow that to start at my age, or I will be an old fossil at 50!

The entry for 29 October 1951 concludes with some reflections on the Foreign Office staff with whom Younger had worked during his period as Minister of State.

... I have got on very well with Michael [Hadow], and he has been a tremendous help to me. As a private secretary & adjutant he is first class – I think his Indian training[70] has made him far better at all that than most F.O. people. On the policy level, he is very good up to a point. Very sensible & efficient & technically competent. On the broad issues he has clearly always been very reactionary – He still is, though I am glad to find that contact with me has shaken him out of a number of ruts ...

My relations with the rest of [the] F.O. have been pretty cordial on the whole. The only senior man I really don't trust is Bob Dixon; I'm sure he is slippery & reactionary. Roger Makins is also reactionary, but far more straightforward. He is formidable and efficient, but somewhat narrow. I was shocked by his recommendation only the other day that we should use military force in Abadan to hold the refinery.[71] I questioned him about it, and found that he seemed to have envisaged hardly any of the obvious consequences and was unable to give any better reason for his view than that he 'just had a hunch' about it.

There are some types of person from whom I might accept a 'hunch' in place of an argument, but Roger M[akins] is certainly not one of them. He is a formidable machine but no artist, & the last person whose unsupported instincts I would trust.[72]

... I much prefer Gladwyn [Jebb], whose political flair is, I am sure, far greater than Roger's. He would not, I think, be a good administrative chief, but he sees things in a bigger way. I have always got on very well with him, & enjoyed working with him.

The one I liked best & trusted most was William Strang. I think he liked me too. He has a much more understanding attitude to social problems than most of the others. I have to admit, however, that he is not a very impressive figure & is not a policy maker such as one might expect from a P[ermanent] U[nder] S[ecretary]. The driving force at present comes from below him & he coordinates & runs the office. His lieutenants are all more formidable than he.

Younger discussed future prospects – for the Conservative government, the Labour Party and Anglo-American relations – in a long letter to an American friend on 11 November 1951. It may serve as a fitting conclusion to this chapter.

... I don't think the Tories will be able to throw over the really important things that we have done. They will do no more nationalisation (nor would we at present) but they will accept most of what we did. Even for steel, I think they will find a formula which gives the government a strong measure of control.

Whatever they may pretend, they will in fact take over from us the idea (which they have strenuously fought) that it is right and necessary to plan the use of the nation's resources, and not merely to rely on the free market. And they will maintain most, if not all, of our social security measures.

In other words, Labour's post-war policy will become from now onwards the orthodox doctrine of the Tories and the City of London! I prophesy that in a couple of years' time, anyone who tries to claim for the Labour Party the credit for any of these policies will simply be laughed out of court!

This may be rather irritating from a narrow party point of view; and it may enable the Tories to stay in power for quite a few years. But historically speaking, it is very satisfactory. It means that the Labour Party has performed the essential task of a radical party in a democracy, by shifting the whole political thinking of the country out of its 19th century groove so that there can be no going back. (It always seems to me that that's what the New Deal did for you[.])

In the process we probably made many mistakes which had to be adjusted. It would have been hard for Labour to make these adjustments, because so many vested interests grow up within a party in power (don't you know it!) but it ought to be relatively easy for the Tories. Their job will be one of tidying up, which they will have to try without going back on any of the major achievements of our government.

In the meantime, I do not think that there is any radical party or group in British politics at all. The communists are negligible at the moment. And the so-called 'left' of the Labour Party, among whom Bevan is the most important, have no programme ready to put before the public. Their leftism is almost wholly emotional, and will have to take a much more practical form, and organise effective backing for itself before it can emerge as a real force.

I count myself in this group and hope to work with them, for I think it is essential to have a genuinely radical force in every parliamentary democracy. Otherwise radicalism is bound to grow up outside the democratic system, either among the communists or (as in France) among the Gaullists or (as in Germany) the neo-Nazis. My guess is that the Tories will retain office for quite a time – certainly for 3 years, and quite possibly for 6 or 8. But in the end they will go because they will make no constructive contribution to Britain's problems and will increasingly fall behind the times. As soon as a renewed Labour party has an up-to-date alternative to offer (which won't be for several years) it will get back to power and will give Britain another shove along the road.

All this may sound pretty academic to you, in view of the plight Britain is in at the moment, and of course all one's theorising could be completely upset by major war or complete economic collapse. On the whole, however, I think we have a good chance of avoiding both.

The economic question, I'm afraid, depends mainly on you. The idea that our periodic dollar crises were due to 'socialist extravagance' etc. etc. was bunk. In fact we did a good job in getting ourselves free of Marshall Aid[73] by the end of 1950. Even that required a terrific increase in production and exports which it would have been hard to maintain.

The rearmament programme and the consequent changes in world prices made our situation once more hopeless. I don't believe that Britain *can* pay its way in the world any more while simultaneously carrying a defence burden on the present scale. We couldn't fight the last war without free U.S. aid; we certainly couldn't fight another without it; and I don't think we can even prepare for another war without it.

On this problem I think Bevan was perfectly right, though I entirely disagreed with his tactics, and thought him wrong to resign from the government. Bevan is not against rearmament in general. All he said was that our programme was bigger than we could achieve and that it was bound to result in our going cap in hand to the Americans. That is exactly what is happening, and I haven't the least doubt that you will have to bale us out to some extent whether you like it or not! It would not surprise me either to find that that you in America start going 'Bevanite' and begin to modify the scale or speed of western rearmament! ...

Of course Bevan's argument has always been based on his belief that we have been over-estimating the Soviet power to launch a really large-scale attack in the next two years or so. The Labour government never accepted that, and nor did Churchill. On the other hand, I think that as the months go by Churchill may modify his view even on this. It is interesting that in his first speech as Prime Minister he referred to a foreign diplomat who, when asked what year would be the most dangerous for peace, replied 'Last year'![74]

I don't know what your strategists are really thinking about this now – (anyway I don't much trust strategists! They are usually so keen to get a big appropriation for defence that they will adjust their calculations to secure that end! That's the same in all countries) – but I think the conviction has been growing in many quarters that the Russians are *not* prepared to risk major military operations. I believe this myself. I believe the Korean venture was not a calculated risk but a mistake. They thought there was virtually no risk in it. Since they found they were wrong, they have been exceedingly careful in the Far East, Middle East and in Germany.

If this view is right, then there would be nothing lost and much gained by, say, extending the present defence programme over five years instead of three. It would relieve the strain on raw materials and enable Britain to use more of her resources for exports and less for defence. It would, I suppose, do something to slow up inflation in [the] U.S. and elsewhere.

Anyway, I think something like this will have to be done unless [the] U.S. is prepared to renew her non-military economic aid to [the] U.K. and Europe on a giant scale. I imagine that will not be an attractive proposition in [a presidential] election year.

Of course everything I have been saying leads to the conclusion that Britain is no longer in any real sense an independent great power. I'm afraid that's right, and will remain right unless we can eventually put an end to world tension and these huge competitive arms programmes. In a peaceful world I think we *could* pay our way, though it would always be more difficult than it was in the days of cheap food and raw materials. But in a tense and insecure world we can't.

This of course makes U.S.–U.K. relations very awkward. After many years during which Americans have been too touchy about being 'outsmarted' and 'high-hatted' by the British, we are now getting to the point where millions of Englishmen are too touchy about American policies.

This applies to Tories quite as much as to Labour people. Indeed I think one of the shocks which is coming to [the] Tories now they are in power is to find that the predominance of [the] U.S. is not just due to the weakness of Labour Ministers, but is one of the facts of life.

You may remember the row there was when Admiral Fechteler was named for Supreme Command of the Atlantic.[75] Every true Britain was outraged – and none more than the pro-American Churchill! I was discussing this with one of our diplomatic correspondents here, and he said, 'You know, it wasn't until the British public learned of this appointment that they realised that U.S. steel production overtopped British in 1896.'

I think that was a witty way of stating the undoubted truth that U.S. preponderance has been artificially concealed from the world for at least 30 years or more. I am not sure how far Churchill appreciates it. Even up to the end of the war, when your total contribution was so much greater than ours, Churchill's own experience, and his peculiar relations with [President F[ranklin] D[elano] R[oosevelt], and the start which we had in many of the techniques of war, all tended to conceal the real shift of power. I think he'll find it very different now.

Already some of the right wing press has criticised him for appearing to accept U.S. leadership, in his first speech at the Lord Mayor's banquet this last week.[76] I think that is symptomatic of Tory thinking as a whole. I mention it just as a corrective to the rather common view that the Tories will cooperate much better with [the] U.S. than we did. I doubt if that will be so. Certainly personal relations were cordial and where we differed (as on China) we understood each other's positions. If there is any real change I suppose it may be because at *your* end, the public and Congress will trust Churchill more than it trusted us. If it turns out to be so, I expect Churchill will exploit his position to be more troublesome to you than we were, not less!

Anyway I hope so! That's the one advantage I am prepared to admit he has over Attlee, so I hope he uses it![77]

Appendix

Kenneth Younger's minute on the
Persian Oil dispute, 6 October 1951

This fascinating document presents a serious problem for the historian. Classified 'Secret', its form is that of an official document, but I have been unable to locate it in the National Archives. In view of its reference to a government decision to overthrow the Musaddiq government by means of covert action on the part of MI6, this is perhaps not surprising, but even if it remains hidden in some Whitehall vault or was even destroyed, to whom was it originally addressed and what was its purpose? There is no indication in the document itself and, unlike some other items in the Younger Papers, it does not bear any subsequent annotation in which he sought to explain the context.

Although the document is written in the language of a conventional Foreign Office minute, its often harshly critical tone makes one wonder whether it was intended for the eyes of the Foreign Secretary or even of senior officials. We simply do not know who else saw it at the time it was written. Indeed, it may not have been shown to anyone. The chronological imprecision of the document certainly suggests that it was written without consulting the files. Younger may simply have written it as a memorandum to himself, possibly intended to guide his own actions in the event of a Labour government being returned at the General Election and his remaining in the same post, or simply as a private reflection on what was perhaps the government's greatest failure in the field of foreign policy.

Since His Majesty's Government's policy in relation to the Persian Oil dispute is now being subjected to so many misconceived criticisms, and since I may not have another opportunity of making my own comments, I wish to draw attention to a number of criticisms which I believe to be valid and a number of lessons which I think should be learnt for the future. Although I myself have attended very few of the Ministerial Meetings on Persia[1] and have seldom been wholly in the picture, I do not wish to suggest from what follows that I myself am free from blame. I had various opportunities to form an estimate of the Persian situation, starting with one occasion in the summer of 1950 when I saw the former Persian Ambassador[2] about the Supplemental Oil Agreement,[3] and later early this year when the present Persian Ambassador[4] expressed his views at great length at a dinner party,[5] but I did not give my mind to the matter over a sufficient period to do anything effective.

In retrospect I think we were all exceedingly slow to realise the trend of events in Persia before the crisis was reached. After the critical point, which I take to be the Rasmara murder,[6] I think that our sources of intelligence were still inadequate and our assessment of the situation faulty. I think that we missed two opportunities in the course of March and April.[7] Thereafter I doubt whether anything except perhaps a more statesman-like policy by the United States could have saved the situation.

The principal reason why our advance information was inadequate was the short-sightedness and the lack of political awareness shown by the Anglo-Iranian Oil Company. They were far better placed than anybody else to make a proper estimate of the situation but, as far as I am aware, they never even seriously tried to do so. Sir William Fraser is no doubt a very good businessman in the narrow sense, but on every occasion when I have seen him, either at Ministerial Meetings or elsewhere during these months, he has struck me as a thoroughly second-rate intellect and personality. He has on many occasions explicitly stated in my presence that he does not think politics concern him at all. He appears to have all the contempt of a Glasgow accountant for anything which cannot be shown on a balance sheet. This is an attitude quite incompatible with the responsibilities of the head of a company like A.I.O.C. operating in so complex and unsettled an area as the Middle East. It may well be that the Supplemental Oil Agreement was quite a reasonable proposal when it was put forward, and it may in practice be as favourable to the Persians as a fifty–fifty arrangement. There can, however, be no doubt that it was drawn up in a manner which makes it seem less favourable than the Aramco Agreement.[8] It is quite astonishing to me that when the Aramco Agreement was published even so limited a man as Sir William Fraser did not immediately see the writing on the wall. Since the crisis was reached it is my impression that there has been considerable difference in view-point between the A.I.O.C. in London and the A.I.O.C. in Persia, and I think that this has added to the difficulty which H.M.G. has found in making a correct assessment.

This criticism of the A.I.O.C. does not, however, absolve the Government from blame. H.M.G. hold 51% of the shares and nominate two directors. There is therefore no excuse for the Government not having ensured adequate political direction of the company. I have not fully investigated this aspect of the matter but, as I understand it, it has not in the past been Treasury policy to make any serious attempt at all to use Government directorships for the purpose of guiding companies such as the A.I.O.C. Directorships have normally been used to give rewards for superannuated public servants, and once appointed they have not been expected to take a very active part in the affairs of the company. Indeed had they done so it would have been regarded as undue interference with a business operation.

The two directors in the present instance[9] are in any case not the sort of people who would have been appointed if the posts had been thought to carry with them major political responsibilities.

The late Secretary of State[10] took a very close interest in the welfare aspect of the A.I.O.C.'s operations, and I dare say Mr. Gard[i]ner may have done a good deal in this sphere. I have not however been able to discover that either he or his fellow director have been encouraged to make their weight felt in other ways.

It may be that the Treasury would say that it looks to the Foreign Office, the Embassy in Teheran and the Consulates in Persia for political advice. No doubt this is quite true, though I do not think it invalidates the point I have just made. So far as the Embassy is concerned, I have never been fully satisfied that it has measured up to its responsibilities either. At every stage of this dispute, as Sir William Strang will, in particular, remember I have kept on complaining that I did not feel we were getting a satisfactory picture of the Persian scene, or that the Embassy were giving us the means to judge accurately the strength of the various political forces operating in Persia. I have throughout had the impression that the Embassy concerns itself almost exclusively with a limited circle of political personalities in Teheran and that its appreciation does not go much deeper than that. While I recognise that in a country like Persia it is in normal circumstances the small ruling class whose opinions are politically effective, nevertheless in a tense situation where popular agitation is going on throughout the country, I do not think that mere juggling with political personalities is an adequate instrument of policy. Moreover, even if juggling with personalities were an adequate way of dealing with this situation, it seems that the Embassy was not properly equipped to play this game either. I cannot help recalling that when, very belatedly, it was decided that the only thing to do was to try to pull Mossadeq[11] down and get in Sayed Zia,[12] it was immediately thought necessary to send out some gifted amateurs from England to handle the situation. I think the Foreign Office recognised that this had to be done and that there was no existing machinery in Persia, either under the control of the Ambassador or under 'C',[13] capable of doing the work which H.M.G. required. Indeed I do not know to whom the Foreign Office was really looking for expert advice during much of this time, for I was astonished to learn that the Oriental Counsellor[14] was away from Teheran on prolonged leave at a very important stage in this dispute. For all I know this may to some extent account for the inadequacy of the background reporting in the earlier weeks, but in my view it certainly does not excuse it.

In retrospect it seems that our advisers, whether in the Embassy or in the Oil Company, have constantly under-estimated the determination with which the Persians were likely to pursue their nationalisation plans and have always rated too highly the possibilities of replacing Mussadeq by a personality with whom it would be easier to reach agreement. This, I think, was the view both of Mr. Stokes and Mr. Harriman after spending a brief period in Teheran.[15] It is of course arguable that the calculations of our advisers would have proved accurate but for the effect of United States' policy in weakening British prestige and bolstering up the extremists. No doubt there is something in this view, but it is not the whole answer. In any case the U.S. attitude became fairly clear quite early on, and was presumably taken into account by the Embassy in estimating Mussadeq's prospects in the later stages. From the very first Ministerial meetings of which I had any knowledge there were some members of the Government in London who advised that the strength of political feeling should be taken very seriously and that we should at the very least make a 'deep bow to nationalisation' – the policy later advocated by the Americans. The Minister of Fuel and Power[16] pressed this view, together with the then Minister of Labour, Mr. Bevan, at the first Ministerial meeting I attended.[17] The Minister of Fuel and Power had previously written to the late Secretary of State a long personal letter warning him of his anxieties about development in Persia.[18] Owing to the late Secretary of State's illness, I understand this letter was virtually put on one side. I have not seen it myself and only know of it by hearsay. Whatever the precise terms of this letter, however, I know that a very similar warning was given at the end of a Cabinet Meeting in January, during the late Secretary of State's final illness, by Mr. Bevan, and the Prime Minister then called for a general report on Persia.[19] I myself have no recollection of ever seeing the result of this, presumably because the Secretary of State returned to the Office and I once more dropped out of the scene.

It will be recalled that various alternative types of proposals were suggested for submission to the Persians after Rasmara's murder when Ala was Prime Minister.[20] Only one of these involved acceptance of the principle of nationalisation and it was not recommended. I believe that this was one of the two mistakes which we made after the Rasmara murder. It must have been almost at the same time, or very shortly afterwards, that consideration was given to sending a Ministerial Mission to Persia. I myself was very little in the picture at this time and only know that if such a Mission were sent it was possible that I might be the Minister nominated. I never knew precisely why this proposal was turned down. I think it would have been futile to send a Minister unless he had been allowed to make imaginative proposals accepting nationalisation. If he had been able to do this, however, before the Mixed Oil Commission had been set up by the Persians,[21] I think there was at least a chance that the situation might have been saved. I have only recently learned that this was strongly pressed by Earl Mountbatten at the time, but I knew that it was also the view of the Minister of Fuel and Power.[22]

I have so far laid considerable stress on the inadequacy of the advice received by the Government. I do not, however, think that Ministers can escape the major blame in the whole matter. As I have already said, certain Ministers always took the view which I believe to be the correct one. There is no reason why the Cabinet as a whole should not have done the same. I think it is probably correct that in the much bigger issues affecting India immediately after the war, a good deal of very cautious official advice was given, but the Government took its political courage in both hands and acted with speed and imagination, and was vindicated by the result. This is just what we have not done in Persia. What I find most galling about the whole thing is that we have been preaching to the Americans and others the need for imagination in dealing with Asian nationalism, and we have not hesitated to indicate that we know much more about this than they do. In this Persian oil dispute the roles are lamentably reversed.

In conclusion I wish to summarise the two or three lessons which seem to me important. Firstly, I think the Government must take a far closer interest in all major British undertakings overseas in which the Government is a shareholder. I asked many weeks ago for a survey of such concerns throughout the world, and I believe some work has been done on it, although I have not seen the result.[23] There should be no sinecure Government directorships.

Secondly, I think a careful review should be made of our diplomatic and intelligence representatives in the whole of the Middle East. Persia is by no means the first Middle Eastern country in which we have made miscalculations since the war.

Thirdly, we should recognise that the attitude which we showed to Asian nationalism in India and Burma in 1946–47 is one which we have to maintain in other parts of the continent, and that it is over-caution and unwillingness to move, both on the part of the Company and of the Government, which has caused the present Persian fiasco.

Fourthly, as a postscript, I think we should face the possibly unpalatable fact that these events will greatly lower our prestige in the whole of the Middle East. It is probably true now, if it was not already true before, that western influence can only be maintained if it is jointly upheld by Britain, the United States and perhaps France. Whatever we may think of the wisdom of the United States policy in this Persian dispute, they are now up to the neck in it, and we can perhaps save something from the wreckage if we can use this fact to induce them to take some of our responsibilities, particularly of a military nature, off our shoulders in this area.[24]

The overthrow of Musaddiq by covert means did take place, but not until August 1953. The reason for this appears to have been that MI6 and its American equivalent, the Central Intelligence Agency, did not get their act together until then. Indeed, it seems that the CIA may even have been supporting Musaddiq in 1951.[25]

Notes

Introduction

1 Apart from his promotion to head of MI5's alien division, the Younger Papers contain several contemporary documents in which his work is praised by superiors and colleagues.

2 Nuffield Transcript, pp. 4–5, Younger Papers and Nuffield College Library.

3 Younger modestly attributed his appointment to the fact that Noel-Baker's personal secretary had worked with him in the early years of the war and was thus able to recognise a familiar face among the hordes of newcomers to the back benches. See Nuffield Transcript, p. 7, Younger Papers and Nuffield College Library, Oxford.

4 Ibid., p. 8. In the spring of 1946, Younger visited the Soviet Union as part of a mission by the United Nations Relief and Rehabilitation Mission to Europe. See ibid., p. 9.

5 Kenneth O. Morgan, *Labour in Power 1945–1951* (Oxford: Clarendon Press, 1984), p. 406.

6 Younger Diary, 27 February 1950.

7 D.O.(46) 40, 13 March 1946, in Ronald Hyam (ed.), *The Labour Government and the End of Empire 1945–1951*, Part III, *Strategy, Politics and Constitutional Change* (London: Her Majesty's Stationery Office, 1992), pp. 216–17.

8 *The Times*, 5 January 1948.

9 See my essay on Bevin's foreign policy in Gordon A. Craig and Francis L. Loewenheim (eds), *The Diplomats 1939–1979* (Princeton: Princeton University Press), 1994, pp. 103–34, especially pp. 108–17.

10 Thus Britain's GDP per head (in 1990 US dollars) was $6,546 in 1940 compared to $7,018 for the United States. In 1950 it was $6,847 compared to $9,573 (Angus Maddison, *Monitoring the World Economy 1820–1992* (Paris: Organisation for Economic Cooperation and Development, 1995), p. 197).

11 Younger Diary, 4 December 1950. See below, p. 46.

12 Ibid., 28 March 1951. See below, p. 69.

13 Ibid., 23 December 1955.

14 *The Diary of Hugh Gaitskell*, p. 568, entry of 2/3 August 1956. See also Younger Diary, 30 December 1956.

15 Ibid., 6 December 1957, 7 January 1958, 29 August 1958, 9 November 1958, 13 December 1958.

16 Younger Diary, 13 December 1958.

17 Younger Diary, 31 December 1964.

18 The speeches were on 26 November and 16 December 1958 respectively. See H.C. Deb., Vol. 596, cols 489–501; Vol. 597, cols 1041–4.

19 Personal communication from Gordon Marsh, 29 October 2003.

1 To the Foreign Office, February–August 1950

1   Clement Attlee, Prime Minister, 1945–51.
2   The only Minister of State in the Attlee government was the number two in the Foreign Office. Today there are Ministers of State in virtually every government department and more than one in some.
3   James Chuter Ede, Home Secretary, 1945–51.
4   Foreign Secretary, 1945–March 1951, and one of the giants of the post-war Labour government.
5   It set out the government's programme for the new session of parliament and took place on 6 March 1950.
6   9 March 1950.
7   I.e. the legislation to nationalise the iron and steel industry.
8   Vincent Auriol, President of the French Fourth Republic, 1947–54. He paid a state visit to London from 7–11 March 1950.
9   I.e. the Foreign Office.
10 On 11 March 1950.
11 Dr Philip Jessup, an international lawyer, was ambassador-at-large in the US State Department, 1949–53. In July 1949 Fosdick and Case were appointed as consultants to assist him in a re-examination of American policy in the Far East in the light of the imminent collapse of Chiang Kai-shek's Nationalist government in China and its replacement by a communist regime under Mao Zedong.
12 He had been Secretary of State for Commonwealth Relations, 1947–50.
13 Younger's fears concerning the possible repercussions of the Seretse Khama affair fortunately proved unfounded. Seretse eventually returned to Bechuanaland in 1956, with his wife, after renouncing all claim to the chieftancy. He subsequently entered politics, however, and became Prime Minister when Bechuanaland obtained home rule in 1965 and president when it became independent, as the Republic of Botswana, in 1966.
14 The Foreign Secretary was away from 29 March to 5 April 1950 attending the ministerial committee of the Council of Europe in Strasbourg and the consultative group of ministers of the Organisation for European Economic Cooperation in Paris.
15 Younger saw Douglas on 30 March and 4 April 1950. See his despatch to Washington, 4 April 1950, FO371/84788/111/G, NA. Together with the Colonial Secretary, James Griffiths, he produced a Cabinet paper entitled 'Chinese Civil Aircraft at Hong Kong' on 3 April 1950, C.P. (50) 61, CAB 129/39, PRO. The Cabinet discussion took place on 6 April 1950. See C.M. (50), 19th Meeting, Item 2, CAB 128/17, NA.
16 On 28 March 1950.
17 Leader of the Conservative Party opposition, 1945–51.
18 Sir William Strang, Permanent Under-Secretary of State at the Foreign Office, 1949–53.
19 For the text of Churchill's speech, see H.C. Deb., Vol. 473, cols 189–202.
20 For the text of Younger's speech, see ibid., cols 207–18.
21 Anthony Eden, the Conservative front-bench spokesman on foreign affairs, 1945–51.
22 For the text of Bevin's speech, see H.C. Deb., Vol. 474, cols 318–30.
23 See above, p. 9, fn. 14.
24 Bevin was sixty-nine.
25 Dean Acheson, US Secretary of State, 1949–53.
26 Robert Schuman, French foreign minister, 1948–53.
27 See below, pp. 13–17.

28 Sir Hartley Shawcross, Attorney-General, 1945–51.
29 Younger was presumably thinking of the communist takeover in China.
30 Bevin went into hospital for a minor operation on 11 April 1950 and returned to the Foreign Office on 8 May.
31 Signed in March 1948, the Brussels Treaty was a multilateral defence pact between Britain, France, Belgium, the Netherlands and Luxembourg. Despite the formation of the much broader North Atlantic alliance in April 1949, it continued to have a separate existence.
32 Emmanuel Shinwell, Minister of Defence, 1950–1.
33 Hugh Gaitskell, Minister for Economic Affairs, February–October 1950.
34 Dirk Stikker, Dutch Foreign Minister, 1948–52.
35 King Leopold III had surrendered the Belgian army after the German invasion in May 1940. He had remained in Belgium during the war and was accused of collaboration by many Belgians. He was removed to Germany by the Nazis at the time of the liberation in 1944 and the left-wing parties did not want him back as king. His younger brother, Prince Charles, was appointed regent, but on 12 March 1950 a referendum produced a narrow majority in favour of Leopold's return. When this took place in July, however, the threat of wide-spread disorder led him to hand over his powers to his eldest son, Prince Baudouin, who became king upon attaining his majority in 1951.
36 Paul van Zeeland, Belgian Foreign Minister, 1949–54.
37 Albert Devèze, Belgian Minister of Defence, 1949–50.
38 27 April 1950.
39 For the text of Younger's statement, see H.C. Deb., Vol. 474, cols 1137–41.
40 The executive organ of the North Atlantic Treaty.
41 A full selection of the British documentation on the preparation of the Anglo-American and Anglo-Franco-American talks, including the official discussions and the inter-ministerial meetings referred to by Younger, may be found in DBPO, Series II, Volume II, pp. 1–267.
42 9–10 May 1950.
43 Sir Roger Makins, Deputy Under-Secretary of State at the Foreign Office, 1948–52.
44 John J. McCloy, US High Commissioner in Germany, 1949–52.
45 General Sir Brian Robertson, British High Commissioner in Germany, 1949–50.
46 In his interview with Richard Rose in 1961, Younger said that he had discussed this matter with Ernest Davies, the Parliamentary Under-Secretary of State at the Foreign Office. It was presumably Davies, therefore, who dissuaded him. See Nuffield Transcript, p. 23, Younger Papers and Nuffield College Library, Oxford. There is no mention of this incident in Davies' own memoirs. See Ernest Davies, *Random Recollections of a Journalist and Politician* (privately printed, 1987).
47 The US administration, and Acheson in particular, were under constant and bitter attack from right-wing Republicans for having 'lost' China and for being 'soft on Communism'. One of the leaders of this campaign was Senator Joseph McCarthy, who alleged on 9 February 1950 that there were fifty-seven card-carrying members of the Communist Party employed by the State Department.
48 DBPO, Series II, Vol. II, pp. 267–74, 276–81, 284–94; FRUS, 1950, Vol. III, pp. 1018–33.
49 Dean Acheson, *Present at the Creation* (New York: Norton, 1969), p. 384.
50 Notes on the Diaries, p. 58, Younger Papers.
51 I.e. not to hand them over immediately to the Chinese communist government. See above, pp. 9–10.

52 Since 1948, Malaya had been the scene of a communist-led guerrilla campaign against the British colonial authorities. The bulk of the guerrillas and their supporters came from the local overseas Chinese community.

53 The question to which Younger was referring here is that of Chinese membership of the United Nations Organisation. When the latter was set up at the end of the Second World War, General Chiang Kai-shek's Nationalist China was not only a member, but also one of the five permanent members of the UN Security Council, along with the United States, the Soviet Union, the United Kingdom and France. Now that the Nationalists had been forced to leave the Chinese mainland for the island of Formosa, the new Chinese People's Republic naturally wished to inherit China's seat in the United Nations. The United States, however, was adamantly opposed. The British government's position at this time was one of abstention.

54 The Soviet Union began a boycott of the Security Council on 13 January 1950 in protest at the exclusion of communist China. It returned on 1 August, after the outbreak of the war in Korea.

55 I.e. the mid-term elections of November 1950.

56 Younger minute, 11 May 1950, Younger Papers. This document is also printed in DBPO, Series II, Vol. II, pp. 320–1.

57 Ibid., p. 321, fn. 5.

58 11–13 May 1950.

59 In fact Schuman made his announcement on 9 May 1950, not on the 10th.

60 This was not so. Acheson was told of the plan in the strictest confidence by Schuman in Paris on 7 May 1950. When the British government were informed two days later, Bevin accused the US Secretary of State of cooking up the whole idea with the French and deliberately keeping him in the dark. See Acheson, *Present at the Creation*, pp. 382–5.

61 Konrad Adenauer, Chancellor of the German Federal Republic, 1949–63.

62 According to his memoirs, Adenauer knew nothing of the Schuman Plan until a few hours before it was publicly unveiled. See Konrad Adenauer, *Erinnerungen 1949–1953* (Frankfurt-am-Main/Hamburg: Fischer Bücherei, 1967), pp. 314–15.

63 The Council of Europe was set up in 1949 as a proto-European union. It suffered from the outset from quarrels over its functions and rivalry between the governmental Council of Ministers and the parliamentary Consultative Assembly. On both issues Britain found itself at odds with France. The Council still exists, but its importance has long been dwarfed by the institutions of the European Union.

64 See Jean Monnet, *Memoirs* (London: Collins, 1978), pp. 288–303, and his memorandum of 4 May 1950, printed in Richard Vaughan (ed.), *Post-War Integration in Europe* (London: Edward Arnold, 1976), pp. 51–6.

65 The Petersberg agreement – named after the headquarters of the western High Commissioners just outside Bonn – was published on 24 November 1949 and provided for some relaxation of allied occupation controls in the German Federal Republic.

66 See p. 17 above.

67 26 May 1950.

68 Younger was right. Bevin was absent from the Foreign Office from 30 May to 7 August 1950.

69 See p. 14 above.

70 Sir Stafford Cripps, Chancellor of the Exchequer, 1947–October 1950.

71 Lord President of the Council, 1945–March 1951. Along with Bevin (who disliked him intensely) Morrison was the most senior member of the post-war Labour government under Attlee.

72 Permanent Secretary at the Treasury, 1945–56.
73 Sir Edwin Plowden, Chairman of the Economic Planning Board, 1947–53.
74 The minutes and papers of this committee can be found in CAB 134/293, NA.
75 Harvey telegrams, 1 June 1950, DBPO, Series II, Vol. 1, pp. 129–31.
76 Bernard Donoughue and G.W. Jones, *Herbert Morrison: Portrait of a Politician* (London: Weidenfeld and Nicolson), 1973, pp. 481, 639.
77 The Cabinet's Economic Policy Committee. See the extract from the minutes of its meeting on 23 May 1950, DBPO, Series II, Vol. I, pp. 78–80.
78 Younger note, 2 June 1950, Younger Papers. A version of this paper, without the first three paragraphs, is printed in DBPO, Series II, Vol. I, pp. 148–9.
79 Younger minute, 2 June 1950, Younger Papers. The minute is also printed in DBPO, Series II, Vol. I, p. 147.
80 Unsigned minute of conversation, 2 June 1950, ibid., pp. 135–6.
81 Leslie Hunter, *The Road to Brighton Pier* (London: Arthur Barker, 1959), p. 13.
82 Nuffield Transcript, p. 35, Younger Papers and Nuffield College Library, Oxford.
83 C.M. (50), 34th Meeting, 2 June 1950, DBPO, Series II, Vol. I, pp. 140–4.
84 Paul Reynaud, French member of parliament. He was Prime Minister at the time of the French collapse in 1940.
85 Frank Buchman, an American who founded the Moral Rearmament movement in 1938. A right-wing Christian and anti-communist movement, Moral Rearmament was regarded with considerable suspicion on the left of politics.
86 Part of the Japanese empire until 1945, Korea had been partitioned at the 38th parallel after the war, with Russian occupation forces in the north and Americans in the south. As in Germany, attempts to reunite the two halves of Korea failed and by 1950 the country was divided into two separate political entities under Russian and American influence respectively. The communist North Korean regime took the initiative in proposing a war to 'liberate' South Korea and the Russian leader, Joseph Stalin, was eventually persuaded to support the plan after he had been led to believe that the North Korean victory would be swift and that the United States (which had withdrawn its forces) would not react.
87 France, the German Federal Republic, Italy, Belgium, the Netherlands and Luxembourg.
88 This alternative scheme was approved by a ministerial committee, of which Younger was a member, on 1 July 1950 and accepted in principle by the full Cabinet on the 4th. See C.P. (50) 149, 1 July 1950, and C.M. (50), 42nd meeting, 4 July 1950, DBPO, Series II, Vol. I, pp. 234–8, 247–50.
89 On 26 and 27 June 1950.
90 23 June 1950.
91 A shorthand term for the Council of Europe.
92 Minister of Town and Country Planning, 1950–1; Chairman of the International Sub-Committee of the National Executive of the Labour Party; and leader of the Labour Party delegation to the Council of Europe.
93 Strachey was Secretary of State for War, 1950–1. For his speech at Colchester on 2 July 1950, see Hugh Thomas, *John Strachey* (London: Eyre Methuen, 1973), pp. 262–3.
94 President Harry Truman authorised the use of US aero-naval forces in Korea on 26 June 1950 and that of ground troops on the 30th. The UK agreed to make naval forces available on the 28th.
95 Passed by the Security Council on 27 June 1950, the resolution recommended 'that the members of the United Nations furnish such assistance to the Republic of [South] Korea as may be necessary to repel the armed attack and to restore international peace and security in the area.' See FRUS, 1950, Vol. VII, p. 211.

96 In a statement of 27 June 1950 condemning the invasion of South Korea, President Truman also announced that he had ordered the US 7th Fleet to prevent both a Chinese communist attack on Formosa and a Chinese Nationalist attack on the mainland. The former was of course much more likely than the latter. See FRUS 1950, Vol. VII, pp. 202–3.

97 Nuffield Transcript, p. 37, Younger Papers and Nuffield College Library, Oxford.

98 On 5 July 1950.

99 It should be remembered that the French Communist Party was supported by a fifth of the electorate at this time and the Italian Communist Party by a quarter. In addition the largest trade union movements in each country (the CGT and the CGIL) were communist-controlled. On 30 September 1948 the Political Bureau of the French Communist Party had declared that 'the French people will not, will never wage war upon the Soviet Union'. See Stéphane Courtois and Marc Lazar, *Histoire du Parti communiste français* (Paris: Presses Universitaires de France, 1995), p. 277.

100 Younger minute, 6 July 1950, Younger Papers.

101 Acheson circular telegram, 22 July 1950, FRUS, 1950, Vol. III, p. 138.

102 See below, pp. 72–4.

103 Cripps memorandum, 31 July 1950, C.P. (50) 81, CAB 129/41, PRO; C.M. (50), 52nd Meeting, CAB 128/18, PRO. Later in August a pay increase for the armed services increased the total cost of the rearmament programme to £3,600 million.

104 See below, p. 31.

105 On 28 July 1950.

106 7 August 1950.

107 The American military position in Korea in July 1950 was so bad that the use of atomic weapons to stem the communist advance was considered, even though it was not pursued. See Callum A. MacDonald, *Korea: the War before Vietnam* (London: Macmillan, 1986), p. 39.

108 For Younger's 'vain attempt', see his minute to Attlee, 19 July 1950, Younger Papers and FO 371/83298/FC1024/51/G, NA. The latter copy bears a minute of the same date by the Prime Minister in which he asked the Foreign and Commonwealth Relations Offices to prepare a paper on the subject. The Foreign Office had produced a draft, to which Younger contributed, by 24 July, but Bevin commented, 'I think we had better wait before putting any paper in. Any of these recommendations [i.e. in the Foreign Office draft] means a general war. If we are not careful we might provoke it . . .' On 29 July a Foreign Office official noted that Bevin had discussed the matter with Attlee on the 28th 'and that the latter had agreed that it would be preferable not to produce any paper for the Cabinet on this subject for the time being.' See FO/371/8329/FC1024/51/G, NA.

109 See also paragraph 7 of Younger's minute to Bevin of 11 July 1950, Younger Papers and DBPO, Series II, Vol. IV, p. 48, for an amplification of this point.

110 President of the Board of Trade, 1947–April 1951.

111 Secretary of State for Scotland, 1950–1.

112 Secretary of State for Commonwealth Relations, 1950–1.

2 The United Nations, September–December 1950

1 This was the meeting of the British, French and American foreign ministers which took place from 12 to 14 September 1950 prior to the fifth session of the North Atlantic Treaty's council of ministers.

2 This debate took place on 12–14 September 1950.
3 Younger's guess was correct. The government had a majority of six votes at the end of the debate on steel nationalisation on 19 September 1950.
4 See above, pp. 28–9.
5 See their report to the Cabinet's Defence Committee, D.O. (50), 67, 30 August 1950, CAB 131/9, NA.
6 See C.M. (50), 55th Meeting, Item 3, 4 September 1950, CAB 128/18, NA.
7 See Bevin telegram to Attlee, 13 September 1950, DBPO, Series II, Vol. III, pp. 43–4.
8 See the extract from C.M. (50), 59th Meeting, 15 September 1950, ibid., pp. 58–61.
9 See above, p. 29.
10 On 15 September 1950, the United Nations forces had launched a daring amphibious assault on Inchon, about 30 miles west of Seoul, the South Korean capital, and well to the north of the then current front line around Pusan in the south-east of the peninsula.
11 Australia, Brazil, Cuba, the Netherlands, Norway, Pakistan and the Philippines.
12 Younger's two main speeches on the resolution were in the General Assembly's First Committee on 30 September 1950 and in the plenary session on 6 October. For the texts, see United Nations, *General Assembly, Official Record*, 5th Session: First Committee, 347th Meeting, pp. 11–12; Plenary, 292nd Meeting, pp. 197–8. For a full account of the debate and the text of the resolution, see United Nations, Department of Public Information, *Yearbook of the United Nations 1950*, United Nations: New York, December 1951, pp. 258–66.
13 Hector McNeill, Younger's predecessor as Minister of State.
14 Andrei Vyshinsky, Russian foreign minister, 1949–53.
15 See the extract from C.M. (50), 61st Meeting, 26 September 1950, DBPO, Series II, Vol. IV, p. 153.
16 Except, interestingly, by the British Chiefs-of-Staff, who did not want to run any risk of a conflict with the Chinese. See Anthony Farrarar-Hockley, *The British Part in the Korean War*, Vol. I, *A Distant Obligation* (London: Her Majesty's Stationery Office, 1990), Chapter 10, pp. 203–33.
17 The point was of course that each of the five permanent members of the UN Security Council – the United States, the United Kingdom, the Soviet Union, France and Nationalist China – had the right of veto.
18 A leading Republican, Dulles had been appointed a special consultant to the State Department in April 1950, presumably in an attempt to secure bi-partisan support for the Truman administration's foreign policy. He was later made a special representative of the president with the rank of ambassador and given the responsibility of negotiating the Japanese peace treaty. See below, p. 76.
19 Solicitor-General, 1945–April 1951.
20 On 19 October 1950.
21 Pakistan's minister for foreign affairs and Commonwealth relations, 1947–54.
22 The resolution was eventually passed by the General Assembly on 3 November 1950. For a summary of the debate and the text of the resolution, see *Yearbook of the United Nations 1950*, pp. 181–95. Since Younger spoke several times, it is not clear to which of his speeches he is referring.
23 On 21 and 23 October 1950 respectively. The text of the speech, which was the same on both occasions, is in the Younger Papers.
24 We do not have the date of the speech to the New York state editors, but its text is also in the Younger Papers.
25 In 1948.

26 Speech to the Council on Foreign Relations, 19 October 1950, Younger Papers.
27 Although the Soviet Union had exploded an atomic device in October 1949, it did not yet have a stockpile of deliverable nuclear weapons, unlike the United States.
28 I.e. the United States, the Soviet Union, the United Kingdom, France and Nationalist China.
29 Christopher Mayhew, Parliamentary Under-Secretary of State for Foreign Affairs, 1945–50. He had lost his parliamentary seat in the 1950 election.
30 For Younger's speech, which was made in the First Committee on 26 October 1950, see *General Assembly Official Record*, 5th Session, 1st Committee, 376th Meeting, pp. 197–9.
31 On 27 October 1950. The paper's United Nations correspondent described it as 'one of his most lucid and effective statements'.
32 Gerrit Jan van Hoeven Goedhardt, Vice-Chairman of the Dutch delegation to the United Nations, 1949–December 1950.
33 The Soviet resolution was introduced in the First Committee on 23 October 1950. The Dutch resolution was finally passed in the plenary session on 17 November. For a summary of the debates, see *Yearbook of the United Nations 1950*, pp. 195–204.
34 24 October.
35 Nasrollah Entezam, Iranian ambassador to the United States and head of the Iranian delegation to the United Nations.
36 Secretary-General of the United Nations, 1946–52.
37 See above, p. 37.
38 For Younger's speech on the 'Uniting for Peace' resolution on 3 November 1950, see *General Assembly Official Record*, 5th Session, Plenary, 300th Meeting, pp. 307–8; and for that on Lie on 31 October 1950, ibid., 297th Meeting, pp. 276–7.
39 Warren R. Austin, head of the US delegation to the United Nations, 1946–53.
40 The vote in the General Assembly took place on 1 November 1950. For a summary of the debate, see *Yearbook of the United Nations 1950*, pp. 125–9.
41 Younger's wife and two daughters.
42 See above, pp. 36–7.
43 Tibet had acquired de facto independence from China under its religious leader, the Dalai Lama, in 1913, but Chinese of all political persuasions refused to recognise this situation. Chinese communist troops crossed the frontier into Tibet on 7 October 1950, although this was not officially confirmed until the end of the month.
44 See above, p. 42.
45 The Republicans gained five seats in the Senate and eighteen in the House of Representatives. While the Democrats were still in a majority in the House, the two parties were more or less evenly matched in the Senate.
46 John Hutchinson, British chargé d'affaires in China, 1950–1.
47 Chinese foreign minister, 1949–58.
48 On 24 November 1950.
49 MacArthur telegram, 28 November 1950, FRUS 1950, Vol. VII, p. 1237.
50 Sir Gladwyn Jebb, permanent UK representative at the United Nations, 1950–4.
51 Ernest A. Gross, deputy head of the US delegation to the United Nations.
52 John C. Ross, the third-ranking member of the US delegation to the United Nations after Warren Austin and Ernest Gross.
53 On 29 November 1950 by the Soviet Union.
54 The first British ground troops, elements of the 27th Infantry Brigade, arrived

in Korea on 28 August 1950. At the end of September they were combined with units of the Australian and New Zealand armies to form the 27th British Commonwealth Brigade. A further British Infantry Brigade Group, the 29th, was also sent to Korea in September. At the time of the Chinese offensive, UN ground forces totalled approximately 423,000, including 224,000 South Koreans, 178,000 Americans and 11,000 Britons.

55 General Wu Xiu-chuan, director of the USSR and East European affairs department of the Chinese foreign ministry, 1949–52.

56 General MacArthur was authorised by the US Joint Chiefs-of-Staff on 27 September 1950 to conduct operations north of the 38th parallel, provided neither the Chinese nor the Russians intervened. However, he was only to use South Korean troops near the border with China and the Soviet Union. MacArthur unilaterally rescinded this restriction on 24 October, a decision which received the retrospective endorsement of the Joint Chiefs-of-Staff. In November 1950, the British government put forward a proposal for a 'buffer zone' between the 40th parallel and the River Yalu which would, at one and the same time, provide a more effective line of defence and reassure the Chinese that the United Nations advance was no direct threat to them. Unfortunately the Americans would not agree to it.

57 I.e. the UN advance to the Yalu River.

58 US Assistant Secretary of State for Far Eastern Affairs, 1950–1.

59 The talks between Attlee and Truman took place on 4–8 December 1950. There were six full meetings in all, as well as various other conversations between the two sides. A great many matters were discussed apart from Korea, although the latter was naturally at the forefront of everyone's attention. Extracts from and summaries of the minutes of some of the meetings are available in DBPO, Series II, Vols III and IV, but the full British record may be found in PREM 8/1200, NA. The American record is in FRUS 1950, Vol. III, pp. 1706–88.

60 Sir Oliver Franks, British ambassador in Washington, 1948–52.

61 On 5 December 1950. See Hickerson memorandum, 5 December 1950, FRUS 1950, Vol. VII, pp. 1408–10.

62 Sir Benegal Rau, head of the Indian delegation to the United Nations.

63 On 8 December 1950.

64 Confidential Annex to C.O.S. (50) 206th Meeting, Item 2, 14 December 1950, DEFE 4/38, NA.

65 Lester Pearson, Canadian Secretary of State for External Affairs, 1948–57.

66 Chao Guan-hua, Vice-Chairman of the Foreign Policy Committee in the Chinese Ministry of Foreign Affairs.

67 15 December 1950.

68 19 December 1950. Younger gave a full account of this meeting in a telegram to the Foreign Office, 15 December 1950, FO 371/83309/FC10211/36, NA.

69 The allusion is to the US House of Representatives Committee on Un-American Activities (HUAC), which was set up in 1938 to investigate internal subversion by fascists and communists. After the Second World War the chief target was communism and HUAC held widely publicised hearings and investigations into alleged communist infiltration in both governmental and non-governmental bodies. By 1950 HUAC's activities had begun to be overshadowed by those of Senator Joseph McCarthy, who as a member of the upper house of Congress was not, of course, a member of HUAC. The phrase 'un-American activities' was one which tended to strike a faintly ludicrous note in European circles, which no doubt explains why Younger put it in quotation marks.

70 He had already spoken to leaders of the other main federation, the American

Federation of Labor, in November. His account of that meeting appears in an unpublished portion of his diary entry for 19 November 1950.
71 The site of the United Nations in New York.

3 From Bevin to Morrison, January–March 1951

1 See above, p. 49.
2 On 1 January 1951.
3 Younger's brother-in-law, Major James Stewart, MBE, MC, of the Argyll and Sutherland Highlanders.
4 In a message to Attlee on 9 January 1951, President Truman denied any intention of practising subversion. See Truman telegram, 9 January 1951, FRUS 1951, Vol. VII, pp. 39–40.
5 The new commander of the US ground forces in Korea, General Matthew B. Ridgeway, admitted to serious problems of troop morale in his memoirs. See *Soldier: The Memoirs of Matthew B. Ridgeway as told to Harold H. Martin* (New York: Harper & Brothers, 1956), pp. 204–7.
6 Hong Kong was of course a British colony and indefensible against a Chinese attack. In Indochina the French had been waging a war against communist-led guerrillas since the end of 1946 and had suffered serious reverses in the autumn of 1950.
7 See Younger's minute to Bevin, 5 January 1951, FO 371/92768/FK1071/97, NA.
8 The Commonwealth Prime Ministers' Conference took place from 4–12 January 1951.
9 See Younger's minutes to Bevin, 1 and 2 January 1951, FO 371/92756/FK1022/6/G, NA; and DBPO. Series II, Vol. IV, pp. 281–2.
10 See Bevin telegram, 3 January 1951, DBPO, Series II, Vol. IV, pp. 284–6.
11 Sir Stafford Cripps had been forced to resign in October 1950 for health reasons and was succeeded as Chancellor of the Exchequer by Hugh Gaitskell.
12 Strachey had indeed written a long memorandum to Attlee and Bevin on the subject. See Hugh Thomas, *John Strachey*, p. 264. In an unpublished portion of the diary for 7 January 1951, Younger wrote that he thought Strachey might resign over the issue.
13 Minister of Supply, 1947–51.
14 This document is available on the website of the National Security Archive at George Washington University in Washington, DC. The reference is: www.gwu.edu/~nsarchiv/NSAEBB/NSAEBB14/doc4.htm
15 Karel Kaplan, *Dans les Archives du Comité Central: Trente Ans de Secrets du Bloc Soviétique* (Paris: Albin Michel, 1978), pp. 165–6.
16 See Margaret Gowing, *Independence and Deterrence: Britain and Atomic Energy*, Vol. I, *Policy Making* (London: Macmillan, 1974), pp. 310–16; Robert S. Norris, William M. Arkin and William Burr, 'Where They Were', *The Bulletin of the Atomic Scientists*, November/December 1999, pp. 26–35; Timothy J. Botti, *The Long Wait: The Forging of the Anglo-American Nuclear Alliance, 1945–1958* (Westport: Greenwood Press, 1987), pp. 66, 79–95; S.J. Ball, *The Bomber in British Strategy: Doctrine, Strategy, and Britain's World Role, 1945–1960* (Oxford: Westview Press, 1995), pp. 62–6, 152–62.
17 This information comes from the excellent, but alas unpublished, doctoral thesis of Christian P. Alcock, *Britain and the Korean War, 1950–1953*, University of Manchester PhD, 1986, pp. 204–6.
18 Robert Scott, assistant under-secretary of state at the Foreign Office, 1950–1.
19 See *The Times*, 13 January 1951.

20 On 17 January 1951. For the text, see FRUS 1951, Vol. I, pp. 91–2.
21 For the text of the US draft resolution, see FRUS 1951, Vol. VII, pp. 115–16.
22 Following American pressure at the Attlee–Truman meetings in December 1950, a further increase in the scale and pace of the British rearmament programme was under discussion at this time. It was finally accepted by the Cabinet on 25 January 1951 and publicly announced on the 29th. It involved spending £4,700 million during the period 1951–4. The period of National Service (conscription) had already been increased from eighteen months to two years.
23 Bevan had become Minister of Labour and National Service on 17 January 1951.
24 See the extract from the minutes printed in DBPO, Series II, Vol. IV, pp. 318–21.
25 Sir Benegal Rau gave the details of the Chinese clarification in a statement to the First Committee of the UN General Assembly on 22 January 1951. (For the text see FRUS 1951, Vol. VII, p. 117.) UN forces in Korea launched a counter-offensive on the 25th.
26 25 January 1951.
27 23 January 1951. For the text see H.C. Deb., Vol. 483, col. 41.
28 See the extract from the minutes printed in DBPO, Series II, Vol. IV, pp. 330–3. This was the second Cabinet meeting on 25 January 1951. The minutes of the first meeting may be found in C.M. (51), 8th Meeting, 25 January 1951, CAB 128/19, NA.
29 Lord Chancellor, 1945–51.
30 Viscount Addison, Lord Privy Seal, 1947–March 1951; Lord President of the Council, March–October 1951.
31 Secretary of State for the Colonies, 1950–1.
32 Minister of Education, 1947–51.
33 Minister of Agriculture and Fisheries, 1945–51.
34 26 January 1951.
35 See the extract from the minutes printed in DBPO, Series II, Vol. IV, pp. 335–8.
36 See Franks telegram, 27 January 1951, DBPO, Series II, Vol. IV, pp. 339–41.
37 See Osmond note, 27 January 1951, ibid., pp. 341–3.
38 See Lester Pearson, *Memoirs*, Vol. II, *1948–1957: The International Years* (London: Gollancz, 1973), pp. 306–7.
39 On 27 January 1951.
40 The British government expressed its concern to the Americans about General MacArthur's statement. See Merchant memorandum, 30 January 1951, FRUS 1951, Vol. VII, p. 146.
41 See the extract from the minutes in DBPO, Series II, Vol. IV, p. 331. Foreign Office officials, of course, could and did claim that they knew what Bevin's attitude would have been, but as Gaitskell himself found out, they could not obtain confirmation from the man himself.
42 Philip M. Williams (ed.), *The Diary of Hugh Gaitskell 1945–1956* (London: Jonathan Cape, 1983), pp. 230–2.
43 See Ben Pimlott (ed.), *The Political Diary of Hugh Dalton 1918–1940, 1945–60* (London: Jonathan Cape, 1986), p. 501.
44 This decision was taken on 29 January 1951. See C.M. (51), 10th Meeting, Item 3, 29 January 1951, CAB 128/19, NA.
45 The resolution was passed by the General Assembly on 1 February 1951. Its text may be found in FRUS 1951, Vol. VII, pp. 150–1.
46 See the statement by the Chinese foreign minister, Zhou Enlai, on 2 February 1951, *The Times*, 3 February 1951.

47 See above, p. 57.

48 The paper to which Younger refers was entitled 'Proposed Four-Power Meeting' and can be found in CAB 129/44 , NA as C.P. (51) 33. The Cabinet discussed it on 29 January and 1 February 1951, but Younger is clearly referring to the second occasion. See C.M. (51), 11th Meeting, Item 6, 1 February 1951, CAB 128/19, NA.

49 The question of 'dangerous dates' is a complicated one. According to a brief prepared for the Prime Minister on 17 December 1950, 1957 had been chosen by the Chiefs-of-Staff before the Soviet Union exploded its first nuclear device in August 1949 as the earliest date by which the Russians might have a large enough stock of atomic bombs to make it worth their while to launch a major war. After the Soviet nuclear test, the Joint Intelligence Committee suggested that the date be brought forward to 1956 or 1955, but the Chiefs-of-Staff disagreed. See Brook minute, 17 December 1950, CAB 21/2248, NA. 1954 was the terminal date set by the member states of the North Atlantic Treaty for the completion of their medium-term defence plan and it had in fact been decided upon before the outbreak of the Korean War. Finally, on 18 December 1950, the Chiefs-of-Staff agreed that 'preparations for war should be based on the formula "War probable in 1952; possible in 1951".' See Confidential Annex to C.O.S. (50), 209th Meeting, Item 6, Item 1, 18 December 1950, DEFE 4/38, NA. This followed Field-Marshal Slim's visit to Washington earlier in the month. See above, p. 49.

50 They did however provide such assistance. See Xiaoming Zhang, *Red Wings over the Yalu: China, the Soviet Union, and the Air War in Korea* (College Station: Texas A&M University Press, 2002).

51 See above, pp. 28–9.

52 See above, fn. 22.

53 See the Chancellor of the Exchequer's Cabinet paper, 'Economic Implications of the Defence Proposals', C.P. (51) 20, 19 January 1951, CAB 129/44, NA.

54 Younger minute, 5 February 1951, Younger Papers. The Foreign Office paper, 'Possible Soviet Reactions to the Rearmament of Western Germany', was submitted to the Chiefs-of-Staff under cover of a letter of 25 January 1951. The text of the paper may be found as C.O.S. (51) 41, 26 January 1951, DEFE 5/27, NA. I have been unable to locate Younger's minute in the National Archives.

55 C.P. (51) 43, 7 February 1951, CAB 129/44, NA.

56 See Eisenhower's statement to the US Congress on 1 February 1951, reported in *The Times*, 2 February 1951.

57 C.M. (51), 12th Meeting, 8 February 1951, Item 4, CAB 128/19, NA.

58 Attlee's speech may be found in H.C. Deb., Vol. 484, cols 58–71 and Younger's in ibid., cols 148–58.

59 For a report of the speech, which took place on 16 January 1951 in Berlin, see *The Times*, 17 January 1951.

60 An influential figure in German industry, especially in the area of arms manufacturing, who had cooperated with the Nazi regime.

61 'Hatred and revenge are bad counsellors' was probably the phrase Younger had in mind. See Sir Ivone Kirkpatrick, *The Inner Circle* (London: Macmillan, 1959), p. 251.

62 The issue was discussed in the Cabinet on 1 and 12 February 1951. See C.M. (51), 11th Meeting, 1 February 1951, Item 5, and C.M. (51), 13th Meeting, 12 February 1951, Item 5, CAB 128/19, NA.

63 For the text of Bevan's speech, see H.C. Deb., Vol. 484, cols 728–39.

64 Jenny Lee, Bevan's wife and Labour MP for Cannock, 1945–70.

65 A long-standing friend and Labour Party colleague of the Youngers.

66 On 10 March 1951. Bevin became Lord Privy Seal.

67 Henry John Temple, later Lord Palmerston, was Foreign Secretary, 1830–41, 1846–51; and Prime Minister, 1855–8, 1859–65. Rightly or wrongly his name is synonymous with an assertive foreign policy and 'gunboat diplomacy'. In his interview with Richard Rose in 1961, Younger said that one of the first things Morrison did after his appointment as Foreign Secretary was to send for a copy of a life of Palmerston from the Foreign Office library. See Nuffield transcript, p. 71, Younger Papers and Nuffield College Library, Oxford.

68 See Pimlott (ed.), *The Political Diary of Hugh Dalton*, pp. 501–2, 505–6.

69 Nuffield Transcript, pp. 68–9, Younger Papers and Nuffield College Library, Oxford.

4 The end of the Labor government, April–October 1951

1 Parliamentary Secretary at the Ministry of Supply, 1947–April 1951.
2 On 14 April 1951.
3 On 21 April 1951.
4 For the text, see H.C. Deb., Vol. 487, cols 34–43.
5 The decision in principle concerning the acceleration of the rearmament programme was taken by the Cabinet on 18 December 1950. See the extract from the minutes printed in DBPO, Series II, Vol. III, pp. 381–6. The views of Bevan and Wilson are presumably those summarised under '(b)' on p. 384, viz.

> ... the Western democracies must endeavour to strike a balance between, on the one hand, reasonably adequate defence preparations and, on the other, the maintenance of stable economies and a reasonable standard of living. The Soviet Government would be well satisfied if defence preparations in the West were pushed to a point which brought economic chaos and mass unemployment ...

6 See above, pp. 69–70.
7 Morrison took charge of preparations for the Festival of Britain, which was designed to celebrate the centenary of the Great Exhibition of 1851, in 1947. The Festival was formally opened by King George VI on 3 May 1951.
8 Although 'Iran' was the official name of the country concerned and 'Iranian' the corresponding adjective, the terms 'Persia' and 'Persian' were still widely used in British official circles.
9 On 21 June 1951.
10 Sir Henry Legge-Bourke, Conservative MP for the Isle of Ely, 1945–73.
11 For the text of Morrison's speech see H.C. Deb., Vol. 489, cols 822–33.
12 Preliminary talks on the agenda for a four-power conference on Germany took place in Paris between 4 March and 21 June 1951. See above, p. 63.
13 On 18 June 1951, for example. See H.C. Deb., Vol. 489, cols 30–3.
14 Andrew Boyle, *The Climate of Treason*, revised edition (London: Coronet Books, 1980), pp. 390, 392.
15 The British records of these talks, which took place from 5 and 15 June 1951, may be found in FO 371/92554, 92556–7, NA. Some of Dulles' telegraphic summaries of the talks are printed in FRUS 1951, Vol. VI, pp. 1105–10.
16 Sir Esler Dening was given the rank of ambassador in October 1950 and given special duties with regard to the Far East.
17 Charles Johnston, Counsellor at the Foreign Office, 1951–5.
18 The peace treaty with Germany in 1919 after the First World War.
19 Yakov Malik, permanent Soviet representative at the United Nations, 1948–52. A report of his broadcast, which was actually made on 23 June, may be found in *The Times*, 25 June 1951.
20 Ibid., 7 June 1951.

21 See below.
22 They began on 12 July 1951.
23 On 10 July 1951. *Tribune* was, and still is, a weekly newspaper representing the views of the left-wing of the Labour Party.
24 I.e. of the Labour Party.
25 Special Assistant to President Truman, 1950–1.
26 Dean Acheson, *Present at the Creation*, pp. 506–8. Harriman arrived in Teheran on 15 July 1951. For American documentation on his mission, see FRUS 1952–1954, Vol. X, pp. 92–148.
27 See H.C. Deb., Vol. 491, cols 465–586. Younger's winding-up speech may be found in cols 573–85.
28 *Draft Peace Treaty with Japan* (Cmd. 8300), London, HMSO, July 1951.
29 See below, pp. 83–6.
30 Richard Stokes, Lord Privy Seal, April–October 1951. A businessman whose firm had important connections in the Middle East, Stokes went to Iran on 4 August 1951 in an attempt to break the deadlock in the negotiations with the Iranian government. He returned on 23 August 1951without having succeeded. Averell Harriman (see above, p. 79) left Iran two days later.
31 Mohammad Musaddiq, Prime Minister of Iran, 1951–3.
32 Mohammad Reza Shah, Iranian emperor, 1941–79.
33 On 29 April 1951.
34 Younger minute, 3 July 1951, Younger Papers.
35 See below, p. 101.
36 These were educational gatherings for organisations associated with the Labour Party.
37 The proceedings of the conference were published. See US Department of State, *Conference for the Conclusion and Signature of the Treaty of Peace with Japan* (Washington, DC: US Government Printing Office, 1951).
38 Andrei Gromyko, Russian deputy foreign minister, 1948–52.
39 On 4 September 1951. For the text see *Conference for the Conclusion and Signature of the Treaty of Peace with Japan*, pp. 31–7.
40 5 September 1951.
41 Stefan Wierblowski, under-secretary of state in the Polish foreign ministry.
42 Gertrude Sekaninova, deputy foreign minister of Czechoslovakia.
43 For Acheson's account of this episode, see Acheson, *Present at the Creation*, pp. 545–6.
44 For the text of Younger's speech, see *Conference for the Conclusion and Signature of the Treaty of Peace with Japan*, pp. 88–97.
45 For the text of Yoshida's speech, see *Conference for the Conclusion and Signature of the Treaty of Peace with Japan*, pp. 276–81. Acheson described it as 'simple, honest and brief' (Acheson, *Present at the Creation*, p. 547).
46 For the text of Younger's speech, see *Conference for the Conclusion and Signature of the Treaty of Peace with Japan*, pp. 296–9.
47 For Acheson's account of this episode, see Acheson, *Present at the Creation*, p. 547.
48 For the text of Acheson's concluding speech, see *Conference for the Conclusion and Signature of the Treaty of Peace with Japan*, pp. 307–9.
49 General MacArthur was dismissed for insubordination by President Truman on 10 April 1951. His dismissal gave rise to a bitter political debate in the United States.
50 At the end of the Second World War, the city of Trieste and its neighbouring territory became a matter of dispute between Italy and Jugoslavia. The western powers supported Italy and the Soviet Union Jugoslavia. Even after the quarrel

between Jugoslavia and the Soviet Union erupted in 1948, the Russians showed little disposition to settle the question of Trieste.

51 Negotiations for a peace treaty with Austria (which had been annexed to Germany between 1938 and 1945) had also failed to make much progress since the end of the war.

52 8 September 1951.

53 On 25 September 1951.

54 For American policy in this period, see the documents in FRUS 1952–1954, Vol. X, pp. 173–201.

55 Chairman of the AIOC 1941–1956. See below, p. 98.

56 The 'supplemental oil agreement' was supplemental to the original concession of 1933. The AIOC and the Iranian government had signed it in 1949, but it was never ratified by the Iranian parliament because of nationalist opposition.

57 See below, p. 97.

58 See below, p. 100.

59 Lord Alexander, Chancellor of the Duchy of Lancaster, 1950–1.

60 The Cabinet meeting in question took place on 27 September 1951. See C.M. (51), 60th Meeting, 27 September 1951, Item 6, CAB 128/20, NA. It was the last Cabinet of the Labour government of 1945–51.

61 Vice-Admiral Lord Louis Mountbatten, Fourth Sea Lord, 1950–2.

62 General Ali Rasmara, Prime Minister of Iran from June 1950 until 7 March 1951, when he was assassinated by extremists.

63 For details of Mountbatten's intervention, see Philip Ziegler, *Mountbatten* (London: Collins, 1985), pp. 499–501. According to this account, Mountbatten saw Morrison on 4 April 1951.

64 The Special Operations Executive was set up in 1940 to carry out sabotage and other forms of 'unconventional' warfare, mainly in enemy-occupied territory.

65 Anthony Sampson, *The Seven Sisters* (London: Hodder and Stoughton, 1975), p. 120.

66 See below, pp. 97–100.

67 Labour MP for Blackburn (East), 1950–5.

68 Labour MP for Maldon, 1945–55.

69 The Liberal Party had contested 475 parliamentary seats in February 1950 and polled more than 2,600,000 votes. In October 1951 it contested 109 seats and polled just over 730,000 votes.

70 Hadow had served in the external affairs department of the Indian Civil Service in the run-up to independence in 1947.

71 See above, p. 89.

72 In his interview with Richard Rose in 1961, Younger described Makins as 'the most powerful policy-making official'. See Nuffield transcript, p. 65, Younger Papers and Nuffield College Library, Oxford.

73 The Marshall Aid programme of American economic assistance to western Europe was scheduled to run until 1952.

74 See H.C. Deb., Vol. 493, col. 80. The date of the speech was 6 November 1951.

75 When the American Admiral William Fechteler was appointed Supreme Allied Commander Atlantic (SACLANT) in February 1951, Churchill complained bitterly in the House of Commons, arguing that a Briton should have been chosen. As a result of the subsequent furore, SACLANT's appointment was delayed for a year and Fechteler became US Chief of Naval Operations in August 1951 instead.

76 For a report of the speech, which took place on 9 November 1951, see *The Times*, 10 November 1951.

77 Younger letter, 11 November 1951, Younger Papers.

Appendix: Kenneth Younger's minute on the Persian Oil dispute, 6 October 1951

1 The main Cabinet committee on the Persian oil dispute was not set up until May 1951. Its records can be found in CAB 130/67, NA. The matter was also discussed in the Defence Committee (CAB 131/10) as well as the full Cabinet.

2 Mushin Ra'is.

3 See above, p. 89. The conversation to which Younger refers took place on 7 June 1950. See Younger telegram, 7 June 1950, FO 371/82374/EP1531/20, NA.

4 Ali Suhaili.

5 I have been unable to find a record of this conversation in the National Archives.

6 On 7 March 1951. See above, p. 90.

7 See below, p. 100.

8 The American historian, William Roger Louis, has written of the Aramco Agreement, which was concluded between the Arabian American Oil Company (Aramco) and the Saudi Arabian government in December 1950 and which provided for a fifty–fifty division of profits as opposed to the payment of royalties, that it 'signified as great a revolution in the economic affairs of the Middle East ... as the political transfer of power in India in 1947'. William Roger Louis, *The British Empire in the Middle East 1945–1951* (Oxford: Clarendon Press, 1984), p. 595.

9 Sir Thomas Gardiner (1950–3) and Field Marshall Viscount Alanbrooke (1946–54). Gardiner's background was in the Post Office. Alanbrooke, of course, played a key military role in the Second World War as Chief of the Imperial General Staff, 1941–6.

10 Ernest Bevin.

11 One of the many anglicised spellings of Musaddiq, see below and p. 100.

12 Sayed Zia ad-Din Tabatabai, a pro-British Iranian politician.

13 The codename for the chief of the British Secret Intelligence Service (SIS), also known as MI6. At this time 'C' was Major-General Sir Stewart Menzies.

14 Lancelot Pyman. 'Oriental Counsellors', unlike most Foreign Office officials, were not generalists, but specialists who were proficient in oriental languages.

15 See above, pp. 78–80.

16 Philip Noel-Baker.

17 This appears to have been at a meeting of the Cabinet's Defence Committee on 2 April 1951. See D.O. (51), 7th Meeting, 2 April 1951, Item 1, CAB 131/10, NA.

18 Noel-Baker's letter, which was dated 15 November 1950, is available as an Annex to another paper he wrote for the Cabinet's Defence Committee viz. D.O. (51) 41, 30 March 1951, CAB 131/11, NA.

19 It is not clear from the available minutes to which Cabinet meeting Younger is referring.

20 Husayn Ala, Iranian Prime Minister, March–April 1951.

21 On 13 May 1951. Its purpose was to implement the nationalisation of the Anglo-Iranian Oil Company.

22 There is some documentation in Foreign Office files about the possibility of sending a junior minister to Teheran at this time. The idea apparently originated with Mountbatten, who proposed Jim Callaghan, who was Parliamentary and Financial Secretary to the Admiralty at the time. See Strang telegram, 5 April 1951, FO 371/91526/168/G, NA. The British ambassador did not object to such a mission in principle, but was clearly unwilling to see whatever junior minister was chosen enjoy the kind of latitude Younger envisaged. See Shepherd telegram, 7 April 1951, FO 371/91526/174/G, NA. The idea was then clearly dropped, perhaps as a result of Mussadiq's appointment as Prime Minister.

23 See above, p. 81.
24 Younger Papers.
25 See 'Nigel West' (Rupert Allason), *The Friends: Britain's Post-War Secret Intelligence Operations* (London: Weidenfeld and Nicolson, 1988), Chapter 8; Stephen Dorrill, *MI6: Fifty Years of Special Operations* (London: Fourth Estate, 2000), Chapter 28.

Index

Acheson, Dean: in bipartite talks
    14–15, 16, 18, 19; character 50, 86;
    competency 26, 43, 47, 83, 84
Addison, Viscount 60, 69
Adenauer, Konrad 17
Air Ministry 2
aircraft dispute, Hong Kong 9, 15
Ala, Husayn 100
Alanbrooke, Field Marshal Viscount 99
Alexander, Lord 89
Anglo-American: relations 62–3;
    'special relationship' 4, 58, 82, 94, 96
Anglo-Iranian Oil Company (A.I.O.C.)
    75, 98, 99–100, 101
apartheid 9
appeasement, US accusations of 44
Arab Palestine, union with Jordan 13
Arab states 11
Aramco Agreement 98
Asia: British policy on 38–40;
    nationalism 101; UN ceasefire
    resolution 48
Atlantic community, building of 17,
    18, 20
Atlantic Pact 27, 31
atomic weapons: abolition of 41; use of
    45, 64
Attlee, Clement: character 32, 69;
    competency 31, 92; on foreign policy
    3, 53–4; relations with Younger 71;
    talks with Truman 45–6, 47–9
Auriol, Vincent 8
Austin, Warren R. 42

Bechuanaland Protectorate 9
Belgian delegation, Brussels 13
Bereitschaften 34
Bevan, Aneurin (Nye): on arms
    programme 28–9, 77, 78; character

32, 54, 67; on Persian oil crisis 89,
    100; as potential Foreign Secretary
    68; resignation 95; support for US 31
Bevin, Ernest (Ernie): character 67–8;
    death 72; departure from Foreign
    Office 68–9; endorsement of Younger
    7; on foreign policy 3, 20, 26, 30–1,
    34, 53; health of 13–14, 15, 17, 18,
    19, 54, 100; on US relations 10–12,
    57
Big Five, peace pact 41
Bodnaras, Emil 55, 56
Bridges, Sir Edward 20
Brussels Treaty, Consultative Council of
    13
Buchman, Frank 24
Burgess, Guy 75, 76
Burma 62, 101

Cabinet: on China sanctions 60–2; on
    German rearmament 65; members
    29–32, 69–70; opposition to US
    policy on China 53–4; reshuffle 8–9
Canada 58
capitalism, of US 3
Case, Everett 8
Castle, Barbara 91
Changjin reservoir, counter attack on 45
Chao Guan-hua 49
Chiang Kai-Shek 25, 26, 47
Children's Act (1948) 2
China: communism in 39; diplomatic
    recognition of 10; economic sanctions
    59–63; interest in Asia 40;
    involvement in Korean War 35,
    36–7, 43–51, 52; negotiations with
    62–3; relations with 15–16, 30–1;
    US 'limited war' policy on 53–4
Chou En-lai 44

Churchill, Winston 10, 11, 25, 56, 95, 96
Chuter Ede, James 7, 60, 62, 69
coal industry 4, 17–18, 19–20, 22–5, 27, 29
Cold War 3–4, 17, 26–9, 30–1
colonial policy 9
Commonwealth: dinner party 48; as member of 'third force' 3; Prime Ministers' conference 57–8; on US policy in China 53, 59, 60; split in 31, 54
communism: Asian view of 38, 39; hostility towards 35, 42–3, 44; Soviet Union 3; US perceptions of 30
Communist Fifth Column 28
Communist leaders conference 55–6
Congress of Industrial Organisations, US 50
Conservative Party: enthusiasm for rearmament 31; harrying government 7–8; prospects for 93–4
Coulson, John 51
Council of Europe 17
Criminal Justice Act (1948) 2
Cripps, Sir Stafford 19, 25, 28, 32, 54, 70, 72
Czechoslovakia 84

Dalton, Hugh 25, 60, 62, 69, 72
Davies, Ernest 8, 19, 75
decolonisation 4
defence: debate 66–8; expenditure 28–9, 73, 95; programme, acceleration of 64–5
democratisation, Western Germany 27
Democrats, US 42
Dening, Sir Esler 76
Devèze, Albert 13
Diplock Commission 6
Dixon, Pierson (Bob) 61, 93
Douglas, Lew 9–10
Driberg, Tom 91
Dulles, John Foster 37, 50, 76, 84
Dutch delegation, Brussels 13

East Germany, paramilitary 34
East, economic/political cooperation in 11
economic legacy of Labour Party 94–5
Eden, Anthony 11
elections, US 42–3
Entezam, Nasrollah 41, 49
Europe: economic/political cooperation

in 11; formation of 'United States of Europe' 3; lack of preparedness for war 46; relationship with 4; threat of Soviet invasion 54–6, 58, 64; on US policy in China 58–9, 60

Far East, British/US policies for 8, 9–10, 15–17, 26, 30, 38–40, 57–9
Fascism 1
Fechteler, Admiral William 96
Festival of Britain 74
Foreign Office staff 93
foreign policy, orientation of 17
Formosa: debates on 43, 44; handing over of 46, 49; US involvement in 25–6; Nationalists 15; support for Chiang Kai Shek 47; US policy on 41, 48; US-Chinese clash 30–1
Fosdick, Raymond 8
Four Power talks 63
France: coal, iron and steel industries 4, 17–18, 19–20, 22–5, 27, 29; opposition to German rearmament 34; visit of President 8
Franks, Oliver 53, 81, 83, 86, 87
Fraser, Sir William 88, 98
Freeman, John 72, 74, 77
French delegation, Brussels 13
French President, visit of 8
Fuchs, Klaus 76

Gaitskell, Hugh, 5, 60, 61–2, 69, 72, 73, 74
Gardiner, Sir Thomas 99
General Elections 1, 2, 4–5, 91–2
Germany: allied forces in 66; coal, iron and steel industries 4, 17–18, 19–20, 22–5, 27, 29; contribution of western defence 33–5; rearmament 11, 14, 26, 27–8, 33–5, 63–7, 81, 82
Gordon Walker, Patrick 32, 68, 70, 74
Government directorships 98–9, 101
Grady, Henry 88
Griffiths, Jim 60, 62, 68, 70
Gromyko, Andrei 83, 84–5
Gross, Ernest A. (Ernie) 45, 48, 49–50

Hadow, Michael 8, 16, 93
Harriman, Averill 78–9, 99–100
Hitler, Adolf 35, 86
Home Office 2, 9, 47,
Hong Kong 9, 15, 16, 46, 53, 54
House of Commons 5; debates 7–8, 10–11, 24, 26, 33, 66, 79–80

Howard League for Penal Reform 5
Hunter, Leslie 23

Inchon landings 36
India: foreign policy 38, 39–40
    nationalism 101
Indo-China 39, 53, 54
Iran *see* Persia
iron industry 4, 17–18, 19–20, 22–5,
    27, 29
Israel 11, 13, 60, 61
Italy 28

Japanese Peace Treaty 75, 76, 77,
    79–80; conference on 81–2, 83–7
Jebb, Sir Gladwyn 45, 48, 51, 58, 60,
    93
Jessup, Dr Philip 8
Johnston, Charles 76
Jordan, union with Arab Palestine 13
Jowitt, Lord 60, 69, 89

King George VI: opening of Parliament
    7–8; Birthday Honours list 77; visit
    of French President
Khan, Zafrullah 38
Kirkpatrick, Sir Ivone 66
Korean War 32, 34: ceasefire talks
    53–4, 81; Chinese involvement in
    43–51; military armistice talks 77;
    outbreak of 16, 19–20, 25–6; UN
    resolutions on 35–8, 76–7; US
    involvement in 30
Krupp, Alfred 66

Labour Party: Conference, Scarborough
    90–1; General Election defeat (1951)
    91–2; leadership of 32, 73–4;
    National Executive 25, 78; policies of
    2–3; prospects for 94; 'schools' on
    international affairs 82–3
Lambeth, Southwark and Lewisham
    Area Health Authority 6
Laskey, Dennis 51
Legge-Bourke, Sir Henry 75
Lie, Trygve 41
Llewellyn-Davies, Pat 67, 73
Low countries, fears of German
    rearmament 27

MI5 1
MI6 97, 99
MacArthur, General Douglas 45, 47,
    52, 61, 86

Maclean, Donald 75, 76
Makins, Roger 20, 61, 89, 93
Malaya 15, 39
Malik, Yakov 77
Mao Zedong 10, 36
Mao Tse-tung 40
Marshall Aid 18
Mayhew, Chris 41
McNeill, Hector: character 32, 35, 70;
    as potential Foreign Secretary 68, 74;
    promotion of 7; on Soviet Union 41;
    on US policy 54, 60
Middle East, British prestige in 101
Mixed Oil Commission, Persia 100
Monnet, Jean 18
Montgomery, Field Marshal Viscount 1
Moral Rearmament 24
Morrison, Herbert: as acting PM 73;
    appointment as Foreign Secretary
    68–9, 70, 72; character 78; handling
    of Persian oil crisis 75
Mountbatten, Lord Louis 90, 100
Musaddiq, Mohammed 80, 88, 97, 99,
    100, 101

National Health Service 73–4
nationalisation 100, 101
nationalism, Asia 101
Nazis 1, 35
Nehru, Jawaharlal 40, 43, 53
Netherlands, UN resolution 41
Noel-Baker, Philip 2, 8–9, 89, 100
North Atlantic alliance 28; formation of
    4
North Atlantic Council: commitment to
    66; meetings of 13–15, 16–17, 81
North Atlantic Treaty 18; territories of
    33
nuclear weapons, use of 56

Obscene Publications report 6
oil dispute, Persia 75, 78–9, 80–1,
    88–90, 97–101
'One Way Only' 77–8
Oriental Counsellors 99
Owen, David 70

Paris Conference 24
Pearson, Lester (Mike) 49, 61
Persia, oil dispute 75, 78–9, 80–1,
    88–90, 97–101
Petersberg agreement 18
Pleven, René 13
Plowden, Sir Edwin 20, 21

Poland 84
Pyongyang, fall of 37
Pyman, Lancelot 99

Ra'is, Mushin 97–8
Rasmara, General Ali 90, 98, 100
Rau, Sir Benegal 48, 49, 52
rearmament 11, 14, 26, 27–8, 31,
    33–5, 55–6
Rendel, George 13
Representation of the People Act (1948)
    2
Republicans, US 43
reputation of Britain abroad 9
Reynaud, Paul 24
Rhodesia 9
Roosevelt, Franklin D. 96
Rose, Richard 23, 26, 70
Ross, Jack 45, 48
Royal Institute of International Affairs
    (Chatham) House 5
Rusk, Dean 47

Sampson, Anthony 90
sanctions: China 59–63; Soviet bloc 27
Sayed Zia ad-Din Tabarabai 99
Schuman Plan 4, 17–18, 25, 27, 29;
    French ultimatum 20–4
Schuman, Robert 12; character 13; in
    tripartite talks 16, 17, 18, 19, 20–5
Scott, Robert 57, 76, 81
Sekaninova, Gertrude 84
Seoul, recapture of 36
Seretse Khama affair 9
Shah of Persia 80, 89
Shawcross, Sir Hartley 12, 68
Shepherd, Sir Francis 75
Shinwell, Emmanuel (Manny) 13, 67,
    69, 89, 91
Slessor, Sir John 56
Slim, Field-Marshal Sir William 49
Social Democrats, Germany 11
South Africa 9
South Korea, defence of 36
Soviet bloc, sanctions against 28
Soviet Union: Bevan's views on 12;
    European/US policies on 17;
    expansionism 39; hostility towards
    34–5; imperialism of 3–4, 26–9, 34,
    82; interest in Asia 40; interest in
    Korean War 43, 46; military strength
    77–8; opposition to UN resolution on
    Korean War 35–6; opposition to UN
    resolution on 'United Action for

Peace' 37–8; UN resolution on threat
    of a new war 41, 81
Spanish Civil War 1
Speares, Denis 8
spying 75–6
St George's Hospital 6
Stalin, Joseph 37, 55
Steel Act 7, 8
steel industry 4, 17–18, 19–20, 22–5,
    27, 29
Stikker, Dirk 13
Stokes, Richard 80, 99–100
Strachey, John 25, 54
Strang, Sir William 11, 20, 30, 61, 62,
    89, 93
strategic materials exports 34
Strauss, George 54, 73
Suez crisis (1956) 5
Suhaili, Ali 98
Supplemental Oil Agreement, Persia
    89, 97–8
Supreme Headquarters Allied
    Expeditionary Force (SHAEF) 1

television, medium of 85–6, 87
Thailand, Chinese population in 39
The Times 41
Tibet, Chinese invasion of 43, 44
Tomlinson, George 60, 69
Truman, Harry S. 26, 41, 56, 84; talks
    with Attlee 45–6, 47–9

United Nations: appointment of
    Secretary-General 42; Chinese
    membership 16; departure of
    Communist states 54; resolution on
    Korean ceasefire 48, 49–50, 53–4, 58;
    resolution on Korean War 37–8;
    resolution on threat of a new war 41,
    81; resistance to Korean aggression
    25; setting up of 2, 4
US: Central Intelligence Agency (CIA)
    101; condemnation of China 52–3;
    contribution to Western defence 27,
    28, 55, 56; Council on Foreign
    Relations 38; Economic and Social
    Committee 80; hostility towards
    Communism 35, 42–3, 44, 47–8;
    involvement in Persian oil dispute 80,
    88–9; policy on China 53–4, 59–63;
    policy on Europe 58; policy on Far
    East 9–10, 16, 26, 42–3, 57–9; policy
    in Persian dispute 101; policy on
    Formosa 41; preparedness for war

55–6; support for German
rearmament 34; troops in Korea 25;
UN resolution on Korean War 37–8,
59–60; visit of Envoy 8; war
psychosis 48–9, 50
US Air Force 55

van Hoeven Goedhardt, Dr Gerrit Jan
41
van Zeeland, Paul 13
Vyshinsky, Andrei 35, 41

war criminals, sentences of 66
war, fears of 48–9, 50, 56–7, 64–5
Western defence 26–8; German
contribution to 33–5: US
contribution to 55, 56
Western Europe, foundations for a
federal union 17, 18, 20, 23–4

Western influence in Middle East 101
Wierblowski, Stefan 84
Williams, Ruth 9
Williams, Tom 60, 69
Wilson, Harold: competency 32, 70,
73; on foreign policy 60, 77, 78;
resignation 72, 74
Wolfenden report 6
world politics, 'third force' in 3–4
World War II 1
Wu Xiu-chuan, General 46, 49

Yoshida, Shigeru 85
Younger, George (later Viscount
Younger) 1
Younger, Kenneth Gilmour, career of
1–6
Yugoslavia, break with Moscow 40

www.ingramcontent.com/pod-product-compliance
Ingram Content Group UK Ltd.
Pitfield, Milton Keynes, MK11 3LW, UK
UKHW020907280225
455677UK00011B/284